CHINA

Understanding the Nuances of Chinese business culture

G.L Koller

Copyright © 2019

All Rights Reserved

ISBN: 978-1-950088-14-0

Dedication

To all the amazing people that I have met on the Road less travelled. I took that road, and it has truly made all the difference in the world.

About The Author

My name is Gerald Lee Koller. I am a Real Estate broker in Orange County, California. As the broker of International Home Realty (www.IHRealty.com), my team of over 30 agents and myself have focused on selling real estate, businesses and property to buyers worldwide. How does this make me qualified to write a book? Good question.

Southern California is a melting pot of people from all around the world. Most of Orange county is new and this means over the last 30 years I have welcomed people from almost everywhere to the area.

After meeting and working with so many different people, I have spent time travelling to many countries to see how they live. In 2009, we started to see a large migration of buyers from China. So, the first thing I did is went to China for a month to start to learn about them. I felt I could not learn by reading or watching travel shows, I needed to smell, hear and feel the country and its people to experience the way they live. The only way to really know the culture was to go there. And that what I did.

After many trips and hundreds of hours of talks with Chinese business people I felt it was a good time to share what I learned.

My background is and has been real estate. I bought my first property when I was 18 years old and I have been in the business in one way or another ever since. I spend a good part of my career in the mortgage business and managed thousands of people over the years. Now in my 50's I spend most of my time travelling and visiting countries worldwide and working to train my team on how to best work with foreign buyers and seller. Last year alone I visited 18 countries, hundreds of cities and met thousands of great people.

I hope you enjoy the results. Feel free to let me know. mrjerrykoller@gmail.com

Preface

When I sat down to write this book the thing that kept creeping into my mind was, most people don't really understand anything about the Chinese, their culture or customs. So where will I start?

I wanted to clear up some of the myths and mysteries surrounding the Chinese and how they do business. This book in no way could encompass all that I learned, so I limited this first effort on the ones I though mattered the most and would be most helpful.

It is good to remember that all people worldwide, for all intents and purposes, are the same. We all want the same things and we all do the same things, albeit we may do them a little different. In China they think it is very interesting how fascinated Americans are with burgers and pizza. An American might wonder how the Chinese can eat so many noodles or squid. I have heard Americans wonder why the Chinese take their shoes off before they go in the house, the Chinese don't understand how Americans can walk into their home with dirty shoes on. I could go on and on. These are minor cultural differences and most of us realize that it is just a matter of habits. In Business there are many unwritten rules that the Chinese live by. As you will read, they are very specific and must be respected. If you don't. it can cost you a lot of business. I once made the mistake of leaving a business dinner early and forgot to thank the host. There were many people there and I was not feeling well, so I slid out without thanking the host.

He never forgot and we never did business together after that. A hard lesson. I spent 3 years working on the ideas presented in this offering. It is presented in a simple format with some examples to guide you. I hope you enjoy the information and find it useful. If not of you would like to comment, please feel free to let me know. www.mrjerrykoller@gmail.com

Contents

Dedication i
About The Author ii
Preface iv

Chapter 1 - Why Sell to China..1
Chapter 2 - Enter the Dragon...17
Chapter 3 - Relationships & Credibility............................38
Chapter 4 - Where You Sit Matters..................................57
Chapter 5 – Trust...71
Chapter 6 - The Great Wall of China 85
Chapter 7 - Lunch is Never JUST LUNCH 98
Chapter 8 - The Mouse Chases The Cat........................115
Chapter 9 - The Deal is Never Done 130
Chapter 10 – Fin..143

Bibliography 155

Page Left Blank Intentionally

Chapter 1 - Why Sell to China

It is not every day in our history that we witness the sudden and exponential rise of a nation. Right now, no matter wherever you are on this globe, there is a high probability if you look into your business market, you will find a Chinese businessman. Some of the regions where there is a growing dominance of Chinese businessmen, include the United States of America, the European Union, Hong Kong, Japan, India, and Pakistan; and this is only to name a few major markets.

Before we look into the question of why sell to China, it is essential that we know how this great dramatic event of the 21st century happened. Once an insignificant communist state embroiled in internal turmoil, the country changed its course and also the geopolitical map of the world. In 1078, China was the world's major producer of steel with 125,000 tons. China became the global leader in technical innovation in textile manufacturing, and that was seven centuries before Great Britain became the world leader in textile in the 18th Century. The rise of the country continued during the coming centuries with other innovations like paper, book printing, firearms and the transportation of these goods with the help of the most advanced navigational system in the world. However, every rise has its fall and the same applied to the fate of China; the growing western imperialism led to its unfortunate decline. By the early 20th Century, once a great nation, became a broken semi-colonial country with a huge, destitute population enslaved by the British opium.

The principal ports of the country were controlled by the western imperial officials, whereas, the countryside was subjected to the rule of corrupt and brutal warlords. These things did not stabilize the country, but the already crumbling state was further pushed into despair, by the Japanese Imperial invasion. By the 1920s, China ceased to exist as a unified country.

The people of the country were starved, slaughtered, and dispossessed by the western powers, while the economy of the country was plundered by Japan. As if the mass destruction of the country in real was not enough, the account of China's once glorious, prosperous, dynamic, and leading world power history was totally kept out of the account of prestigious US and British academics.

CHINA

The country was in tethers, broken and destroyed in every sense. However, the world, especially the west was in for a surprise, when the country rose from the ashes, dusted itself, and became the second largest economy of the world. The ascent of communism in China became a blessing for the country and one after another, the Red Army of the country fought with the enemies of the country. First, China took its freedom back, then they took their position in the world economy back. By 2010, China displaced the United States of America and Europe as the leading trading partner in many countries in Asia, Africa, and Latin America.

This displacement of the world's largest economies was achieved by China's sustained growth in its manufacturing sector, highly concentrated investments, technological innovation, high profits, and also by a protected domestic market. As China stepped out into the global markets, the country also opened its doors to foreign businesses, however, their capital profit was always within the framework of the Chinese government's priorities and regulations.

Today, China is ranked as the number one economic superpower in the world, by the IMF (International Monetary Fund), surpassing the ranking of the United States based upon the PPP (Purchasing Power Parity), a useful GDP (Gross Domestic Product) comparator. The data from the IMF shows that China produced 17% of the world's gross domestic product in 2014, exceeding the USA. The country's economic growth performance over the last 30 years has impressed most development economists.

Opportunities In The Chinese Market

If we look at the Chinese market with a business and entrepreneurial perspective, then the country can be described as a land of opportunities. China houses the world's largest population of 1.379 billion people. With the largest population in the world, China is also the second fastest growing consumer market in the world, overtaking Japan's position. It has a private consumer spending of US$3.3 trillion, which accounts for 8% of the world's total. This growth makes way for more consumer products, especially from foreign suppliers as the Chinese consumers equate foreign products with quality.

The hunger of Chinese consumers for foreign brands can be explained, by understanding consumer behavior. The first factor that drives the Chinese consumer is the price discrepancy. The price of luxury products in China is very high, as compared to the foreign manufactured luxury products. The price discrepancy pushes Chinese consumers towards foreign brands and markets. The second most important factor is the authenticity of the products. China is notoriously known for its counterfeits of luxury products. Therefore, consumers tend to avoid the local luxury products.

Apart from the consumer behavior, there are many other opportunities present in the Chinese consumer market. The country has a political commitment to consumption-based economic growth. The political leaders of the country have made increasing long-term consumption goals. They have implemented subsidies on health care and housing, to allow people additional discretionary spending. The consumption of the country is expected to be three times higher in the coming 10 years, due to the increased wages and the urbanization process.

Six Trends In China

Growth and changes in the political standing of a country introduce a number of trends in its economy. The first trend that emerges in the wake of economic growth is urbanization. ***Urbanization*** can be defined as the migration of people from rural to urban areas, which usually act as the center of economic activities. The scale of urbanization in China is without precedent in human history.

The primary reason for this unprecedented urbanization is the economic boom of the country. It is essential to keep in mind that urbanization is not a new phenomenon for China. In fact, its urbanization started almost 4,000 years ago. The growing urbanization shows that China is able to sustain a large population, and the middle class of the country is benefitting from the current economic boom of the country.

The second trend that countries with fast economies show, is the ***heightened manufacturing scale***. In recent history, China has emerged as a manufacturing powerhouse. A country, once in the depths of despair, overtook the position of the United States of America in 2011, as the world's largest producer of manufactured goods. The manufacturing engine of the country has boosted the living standards, by doubling the country's GDP per capita over the last couple of decades. The doubling of China's GDP per capita has given rise to **Chinese consumerism** which is the third trend of a developed economy. Today, the appetite of Chinese shoppers has extended well beyond the borders of their geographical borders. The Chinese consumers have been known to have a preference for foreign luxury products, such as Swiss watches and high-end handbags.

There is a Japanese term *"bakugai"* that was created to describe the explosive shopping spree of the Chinese tourists. This spending spree of the Chinese consumers is not without its influence, but it has great sway on many of the global fashion labels. The author of the *As China Goes, So Goes the World*, Karl Gerth, writes that the Chinese consumerism is transforming everything.

He further states that the Chinese population is following the Chinese dream which is the American dream plus 10%. The question that arises from taking a look at Chinese consumerism is how the Chinese consumers can shop in foreign markets with such ease. The answer to this question is that the ***currency of the country*** makes the consumerism a viable practice. China's Yuan is expected to become one of the world's strongest currencies.

The strength enables people to spend on foreign luxury products, and continue to grow their standard of living. The strength of the currency is due to the well-established banking system and the foreign exchange reserve. The country has a total of $15 trillion in bank deposits, and this amount is growing by2 trillion every year. And the foreign exchange of the country amounts to a total of $3.5 trillion.

This increasing amount of bank deposits and the growing foreign exchange can be attributed to the people of China, who are not there to just consume, but they are the ones making such consumption even possible. ***Brain power*** is the ultimate resource of any country for its growth. The growing population of China is also producing a greater number of college graduates.

In 2012, the country produced 7.5 million graduates, making the Chinese brainpower another game-changing phenomenon. China is known for providing low-cost products and when it comes to brainpower, China keeps on fulfilling its long-lasting promise of providing cheap skills. Chinese engineers cost far less than their American counterparts.

Single-degree engineers in China generally make up to $4,800 to $8,800 a year, depending on experience and the company, including payments to housing, pension, and medical funds that can raise the compensation figure by 50 percent. The research and development (R&D) of the country matches its ambition. The investment of China in its research and development amounts for 2.2 percent of the world's research and development spending.

The growth of this country is not centered in one direction, but it is diversified. And in 2011, China surpassed Japan and is now second only to the United States. The manufacturing companies in China operate in a very favorable environment with massive scale, deep pockets, and access to large numbers of skilled professionals. For instance, Cisco has 66,000 employees but only 21,000 in R&D, Huawei has a workforce of 150,000, of whom 68,000 are in R&D.

In this globalized world, growth and prosperity of an

economy are impossible without the phenomenon called the internet. The *Internet* has played an important role in the globalization of the world, by removing the physical and geographical boundaries. However, when it comes to China, like everything else, they are on a different path as compared to the rest of the world in the sense of internet. If you are living in this advanced age, the internet has great involvement in your daily life. Then, you should be aware of all the aspects of the modern internet which includes: Google, Facebook, LinkedIn, SnapChat, Instagram and Whatsapp. But when you enter China, the internet that you know changes; Facebook and Google are not used in the country.

People use Baidu, 360 Search, and WeChat or Weixin (微信). Amongst the three, WeChat is the most popular mode of connectivity and its revolutionary features have changed the way of Chinese life. This app has allowed people to leave their wallets at home, as they can pay through their WeChat account to a number of businesses.

Around 600 million WeChat Pay accounts are active, with restaurants, clothing stores, street food vendors, and even homeless beggars are turning to WeChat QR codes to replace cash and bank cards. However, the new phenomenon of the internet has become the center of the modern lives of people in China. From online businesses to the growing online consumerism in China, every trend proves the above statement.

E-Commerce In China

The E-commerce of China has given the world companies like Alibaba and businessmen like Jack Ma. The e-commerce market of the country continues to see double-digit growth year, after year. China is home to 730 million internet users; it accounts for 40% of global retail e-commerce, and its mobile payment market is a whopping eleven times the size of the U.S. market. The Singles' Day on 11th November is a popular shopping holiday. On this day, when single people in China celebrate, is the epitome of consumerism in the country.

The day also shows why China's consumption-led economy is evolving digitally. On November 11, 2017, the e-commerce giant Alibaba saw sales growth of 39% in comparison to the event in 2016, suggesting that Chinese consumers are confident in their spending and that consumption will continue to rise in the future. The increased online shopping preference amongst Chinese consumers has increased the competition in the e-commerce market. Due to the increased competition, there are multiple e-commerce companies in China, for instance: Alibaba, Taobao, JD.com, and Pinduoduo.

In the Chinese e-commerce market, advertisement is very important. Because companies in this marketplace are fighting for market share from large businesses like Alibaba, they need to stand out and reach their target audience at the right time. Therefore, internet advertisement in 2017 amounted for 290.27 billion RMB (Renminbi), and mobile advertisement accounted 60.29% of that number.

For an entrepreneur, who wants to enter this market, it is essential that they know the significance of WeChat. It is at the center of the e-commerce industry of China, from online payments to online advertisements, it is enabling both businesses and consumers at the same time. Another form of advertisement used by marketers in China, is the news feed advertisement.

Newsfeed advertisement is not a new phenomenon for the marketers in the international arena. But in China, it is a new phenomenon because such advertisement uses

Facebook as its primary platform, which is not available to Chinese consumers. However, companies like Baidu have launched news feed advertisement products on the PPC (Pay Per Click) platform.

A growing economy needs stable social grounds to stand on. If the population is not well-fed, educated, and does not have employment opportunities, then such a country can never grow economically or otherwise.

Education And Health Care Industry In China

China's education system is its most powerful weapon. Knowledge is power, and China is a great example of how this phrase is hundred percent true. It has the world's largest education sector, and in 2012, it had nearly 200 million full-time students. China's education system is a great attraction for international educational institutions, because the Chinese education system is struggling to meet the needs of the people.

Traditionally, Chinese people have been highly appreciative of the role of education in development. This appreciation is highly reflected in the educational expenses of the country, as it comprises a large proportion of the income expenditure of households. After education, the second most important social pillar in China is healthcare.

Since China has the largest population in the world, healthcare companies have capitalized on this large market. The local companies have also improved their technology, and research and development efforts. China is also the focus of big pharmaceuticals around the world, because of the low cost of developing drugs. For instance, a drug that is developed in the United States of America costs $3 to $4 billion, whereas the same drug can be developed for $30 to $40 million in China.

Tourism Industry In China

Today, the phrase that China is the largest something is very common, and when it comes to tourism, it is close to becoming the largest industry for it too. China is the second largest country with thousands of years of history, which makes it a great tourist attraction. There are many investments opportunities in the Chinese tourism industry, especially during the Chinese touristic peak season, also known as the *"Golden weeks."* The tourism industry represents a big part of the country's economic growth. This industry has already outperformed other large industries, such as banking and automobile manufacturing.

Import And Export In China

Trading is what China is known for, and it is also the major contributing factor which aided in the country taking its global position of superpower back. It is the world's second largest trading nation, coming second only after the United States of America. For many countries around the world, China is rapidly becoming their most important bilateral trade partner. In 2011, they were the largest exporting and importing partner for 32 and 34 countries, respectively.

In the recent years, the Chinese government has focused on reducing their exports and increasing their internal consumption. The primary exports of the country include: electrical and other machinery like data processing equipment, apparel, radio telephone handsets, textiles, and integrated circuits. The primary imports of the country include: electrical and other machinery, oil and mineral fuels, optical and medical equipment, metal ores, and motor vehicles.

At the beginning of this chapter, we informed that we will answer the question of why sell to China, later. And the answer to this question is very simple: the country has a large growing and financially able population with a preference for foreign products. And when it comes to doing business, all you need is demand and a target market that can afford the price. So here it is, the whole chapter states the reason why you should sell to China.

China is the story of rise and fall, and then rise again. The country has one of the oldest cultures in the world, and today it is a cause of concern for many European powers. It also represents a threat to the unchallenged supremacy of the US. However, the country is an economic marvel mostly, because it emerged from such ruinous condition that no other country or nation would have been able to do. In this chapter, we looked at the question of why sell to China, and in the next chapter, we will see how you can enter the lair of the Dragon (China).

Chapter 2 - Enter the Dragon

Being the world's most populous country, China is immensely diverse and rapidly changing over time. Its economic success and prosperity have improved the quality of life of millions of people and for all of us, in general. Its culture stretches back to 4,000 years and has served as the foundation of the modern world. Not only does the country's regions comprise of distinguished cultures, but there are also numerous historical, geographical, and climatic differences contributing to its celebrated diversity.

This creates a sense of mysticism in the way China has represented itself in its uniqueness. What is more fascinating about China is the fact that this country that spreads on the vast expanse of over nine million square kilometers of the globe, lays out an array of possibilities not just for its citizens, but for the foreign visitors and expatriates, too. As a result, it stands out to be one of the most visited tourist and business destinations.

China is incredibly exotic and rich in its distinctiveness. It offers countless opportunities, new experiences with a new way of living, and a learning ground extracted from its rich cultural heritage. Its architecture and modern infrastructure are also remarkably striking. Moreover, Chinese customs and traditions which include their music, art, language, literature, food, and clothing, all display their exclusive creativity and diversity.

China has its culture and civilization deeply rooted in itself, and has managed to influence its neighboring countries greatly. Many countries have had the impact of the Chinese civilization in their process of development. In this chapter, we will study more about what lies within this dynamic and vibrant cave of treasures, and what life in China is truly like.

Lifestyle In China

Life in China can be an overwhelming experience, as it is one of the largest and the most populated countries with diversity on such a large scale. China has progressed in quality of life over the years, which enables the citizens to enjoy a higher standard of living.

We all are well aware of the importance of education in the prosperity of a nation. China has taken this seriously and started providing improved educational facilities, which is the basic reason for its constant progress. The years of continuous economic struggle have resulted in a significant improvement in the life of both women and children. Their status has upgraded drastically.

Due to an increased number of aged Chinese citizens, the government has given access to designated senior care and protection. Therefore, in terms of lifestyle, Chinese society has become relatively more self-sustaining and accommodating in the current age. According to culture and tradition, the family is primarily considered to be the microcosm of the Chinese society. The family has always been the source of support, livelihood, and security in the past Chinese culture.

Therefore, it would be correct to call the Chinese society more family-oriented, as most of the Asian cultures are. It lays emphasis on the importance of family to the extent that extended families still exist in the country. These extended families usually include the grandparents, parents, and their children. The parents may be found working and financially supporting the children and their own parents, whereas the grandparents may spend their time taking care of the young ones. This is also found in other countries that prefer adhering to their old societal norms and values. As represented in the conduct of the life of Chinese people, their culture sticks to the principles of Taoism. It is something clearly visible in the worldview and traditions upheld by the Chinese population. Taoism is considered more than a religion or a philosophical perspective that teaches to embrace the simplicity in everything, and pursue harmony with nature.

In addition to nature and simplicity, festivals too, are kept in high regard in the Chinese culture. They are always celebrated with great fervor and enthusiasm. Even though festivals are one way that the Chinese traditions emerge to be noticeable on the global canvas, bits and pieces of these traditions can be observed in the ordinary lifestyle and activities of the Chinese.

This celebrated string of traditions is visible in music, art, literature, and the overall approach to worldly circumstances, such as social interactions that the Chinese hold. Therefore, it is quite clear through their lifestyle that they have carried forward their traditional Chinese values and virtues, despite the changes in global dynamics and worldwide culture. It is not unusual to find some old neighborly men playing chess, near a newly constructed building in the area. The country is an exciting mesh of the conventional and the modern; which is all tied together with their dominant culture. This, however, does not mean that these people are resistant to change. They are often more than willing to embrace new concepts and ideas for their own advancement. China's economic success has resulted in providing comfortable living standards, raises in salaries, and other facilities that can make us consider the country to be more lavish than many western countries.

People in China are relatively friendly and polite. They have a warm and welcoming attitude towards foreign visitors. The Chinese display their culture openly, without any inhibitions, throughout their everyday lifestyle. Regardless of the railroads, metro stations, and new architecture, the local people of China continue to integrate their traditional lifestyle into the modern developments happening around them. You may even find people carrying out casual conversations in the public setting.

The rural life of China is comparatively low-paced to the urban life of China, which is fast-paced. Therefore, for foreign visitors who wish to live a similar life than they live in the west, they should reside in cities like Shanghai or Shenzhen. Shanghai, has a permanent population of over 24 million (The Guardian, 2015). It is one of the major cities of China. The place is packed with modern architecture and skyscrapers.

Perhaps, it is the ideal place for people who crave the razzmatazz and hustle bustle of city life. Shanghai is the epicenter of business and commerce in China, offering a broad spectrum of opportunities for people who wish to pursue corporate and commercial activities in the country. This city is also considered to be a well-established artists' hub, with a nightlife that acts as a constant source of tourist attraction.

Shanghai can more accurately be considered a unique blend of Chinese and Western cultures. Similarly, Shenzhen with a population count of over 12 million people also stands distinguished as an international business nucleus for the country. The city majorly deals with exports and imports between local and foreign industries, drawing in business enthusiasts from all over the world, looking to establish business grounds in the country of the dragon. Like Shanghai, Shenzhen is a modern city, which is progressing on many levels and offers a lifestyle full of opportunities. The local language is a very important part of the country. Not just for being a means of communication, but a way of representing itself. Similarly, China also considers language to be of high importance.

In China, most people do not speak English, but cities like Shanghai, Shenzhen, Beijing, and Guangzhou have a majority of people interacting in English. This is also because of the westerners who have migrated to this country, and have now settled here. These westerners may include businessmen, vacationers, or students who have come to explore this place.

The level of modernity varies as you glance at the different regions in China. And although the majority of the population can now speak English, it does not remove the language barrier between local and foreign people. Besides language, you will experience a lot of noise in China. People are accustomed to talking loudly. This might be a little odd for westerners, as they have a habit of talking in a lower tone, unlike the Chinese people.

The locals may say that the reason for it is that they have a big country, and they have to speak loudly to communicate in a better way. You may experience this in restaurants when you go out to dine. You have to yell at the staff of the restaurant, in order to grab their attention. If you are unable to do so, they may not respond to what you are saying. So, this manner of speech may come off as rude and contradictory to good etiquettes, but it is a part of Chinese culture. Another prominent aspect of Chinese lifestyle is the traffic on the roads. Particularly in cities like Beijing and Guangzhou, traffic is overwhelmingly massive.

This is due to the high population of these cities. What is more unappealing is that the driving standards of people are as bad as the overwhelming traffic. However, the good thing about this is that no matter how dangerous one may think driving can be on the roads of China because of traffic, the vehicles are generally moving at a very slow pace because of less space for cars to move forward, reducing accidents. People do not line up in a queue to wait for their turn, when on a bus or train. Rather, they may tend to rush to avoid missing their turn or their spot.

However, the most appreciable thing about the Chinese people, regardless of their impatience and distinguished etiquettes, they hold a lot of respect in their hearts for the disabled, elderly, or pregnant passengers, as they leave their seats for them. Yet, you may be squeezed if you are not one of those, and it can be worse for you if you plan to go out during rush hours. Even though these habits and behavioral patterns may seem annoying and disturbing to us, our intention is not to scare you away by these facts. These problems should not discourage you from visiting such a beautiful country.

Even if there may be no other reason as appealing to encourage you to visit, the Chinese cuisine is enough to pull you to itself. The flavors are diverse, ranging from spicier dishes of Szechuan and Hunan, to a milder taste in Shanghai cuisine. It's unique and delicious and has attracted people from all over the world due to its tantalizing uniqueness. Therefore, the aim is to present China as it is and to help you embrace the differences in culture, etiquettes, and learn more about what this amazing place.

China's Source Of Income

Fifty years ago, China was struggling as a nation. It was suffering from hunger and poverty, but it has now emerged as the world's largest market economy, in terms of its products and services. It plays a vital role as a manufacturer and industrial producer, in the global market. China's manufacturing and industrial sectors alone account for around 40% of the country's GDP. It determines the amount of income a country makes through its goods and services.

Furthermore, the country is also ranked as the world's largest exporter and the second largest importer. This has resulted in a faster-growing consumer market, which is increasing the country's income and also providing employment to millions of people. Let's look at the avenues of earning that make China such a developed nation.

Manufacturing

China manufactures its goods. It sells these goods and provides related services more than any other country. The goods it produces ranges from computers, broadcasting equipment, integrated circuits, textiles, cement, chemicals, electronics, cars, ships, aircraft, rails, and toys. It leads in the manufacturing sector due to its production of a variety of goods. For instance, around 80% of air conditioners in the world are created by Chinese companies, and the country has produced 45 times more computers than produced by all other companies combined. It also has a huge industry of cell phones which are exported to other countries worldwide. China also stands as the third-largest automobile manufacturer, even though they have not received much credit as compared to countries, like Sweden, Japan, or the USA.

Agriculture

Another source of China's income is its agricultural industry. Although statistics demonstrate that Chinese farms are the least productive when compared to other countries, due to the unfavorable climatic conditions. However, it does serve as an integral source of income for China. There are almost 300 million farmers in China, which are more than the population of most countries in the world. The staple crop which is largely produced in China is rice. The country also produces wheat, tomato, fish products, potatoes, peanuts, corn, soybeans, oilseeds, and tea. Vegetables, fruits, and meat are also exported to other regions and neighboring countries.

Other Services

A successful services sector points to the wealth of a country. According to a study in 2010, the Chinese services sector was found to be 43% involved in the total Chinese production, which is still less when compared to its manufacturing industry. Also, there are more people employed in the agricultural sector, as compared to the services sector. Nevertheless, China has still improved in the provision of services over the years. For example, in 1978, before the economic reform in China, there were no signs of shopping malls and private retail markets.

But now with the rise of markets, tourism has increased as well. Big foreign companies such as Microsoft have become a part of China's services sector. This has resulted in the rise of the telecommunications and the e-commerce industry. There are also various strategic industries, such as information technology and biotechnology that are considered to be of high importance. In addition to that, the healthcare sector of China is the fastest-growing health sector in the world.

Housing In China

The income of a country regulates the standard of living of its citizens, since the income and the cost of living are interdependent. The standards of living and the housing prices in China vary from region to region. For example, housing prices in Beijing and Shanghai are relatively higher than the more, rural areas. Therefore, only rich people can afford to enjoy a higher standard of living. Nevertheless, Chinese banks have begun to offer mortgages, which is enabling families to get their own place to live.

Back in the day, China had apartments that were crowded with extended families living together. They worked, socialized, ate, and slept in the same place. However, many Chinese cities have undergone a spatial transformation over the years. Poor neighborhoods have been changed into luxury housing and shopping malls. This development has improved the overall standard of the people, and the competitiveness of the cities, although the factor of affordability remains constant for people with less income.

Immigrating to China is ideal for expatriates, who like the city life and its hustle bustle. This is also beneficial if they want to pursue their career, while living in a country that offers so many opportunities. For expats, there are various kinds of accommodation, ranging for small apartments to huge villas which they can find with the help of any real estate agent. Cities like Beijing, Guangzhou, and Shanghai are popular among expatriates due to their modernity, and economic and political influence. Guangzhou is also popular, due to its low cost of living. However, other cities such as Shenzhen, Suzhou, and Tianjin are gaining recognition too.

The houses in China provide utilities like water, electricity, and gas to residents, but there are various plans that need to be adhered to. Facilities like heating have a fixed time. There are deals and packages for internet connections and phone calls although, some websites may be inaccessible. In a nutshell, housing in China has progressed over the years and serves as an excellent means to live for the citizens and foreign visitors.

Work Life In China

Although there have been many issues in China and it has undergone many transformations in its history, there are still millions of people who are working here, that have come from abroad. In China, you will find people who work and carry out their day to day chores very passionately. Their work ethic is based on their culture, which brings out their positivity and keeps them focused.

The government also encourages citizens and foreign workers to work hard, and it refuses to give any support to unproductivity and unemployment. This is a reason why people are motivated to work for themselves, and save money for their retirement. Chinese people are very humble as they do not consider any job to be shameful. They are very zealous to participate in any kind of work they are assigned, if it helps them to earn money for themselves.

Chinese people work with a lot of enthusiasm and are willing to work hard even in the most hectic jobs. The working hours in China are between 08:00 to 18:00 which makes the average shift to be ten hours long. But as in the case of industries and factories which clearly require more time, two hours of break must be provided to adjust the work hours.

Therefore, on a weekly basis, the working hours make up to 50 hours. There is also high competition in the job market in China which makes it difficult for people to get a job, unless they have capabilities that make them stand out from others or better academic qualifications. In an attempt to save money for retirement, many people tend to spend long hours at work. They may put off vacation and their goals in the expectation of achieving them, once they're done saving money till the time of retirement.

Therefore, to have a prosperous career, a balance needs to be created between the job and the social life, if you are working in China. Although working overtime will get you extra money, it is going to snatch away the comfort of spending time with your family and friends. Hence, it is advised to distribute your time accordingly, between workplace and personal life. Chinese people do value family and friendships a lot. We can see it through their friendly behavior and peaceful culture. Their family holds more importance than any other thing.

CHINA

There is no national minimum wage in China. Each province or region sets their own minimum wage, which sometimes complicates matters. Wages are also increased according to the cost of living. This has raised the standards of living for the people, and helped them to discard their old ways of living. Moreover, there are only seven public holidays which gives people less time to spend off from the stress of work. This leaves little room for people to go on vacations, which may sometimes cause unhappiness.

People spend most time at their workplace and are not able to live their life, the way they may have dreamed. Regardless of the stress and challenges, the work life in China is productive and helps in accomplishing ambitious career goals. The environment fills you with enthusiasm for work; and this friendly environment, despite the hard work, makes working in China worthwhile.

The Impact Of Economic Expansion On Chinese Lifestyle

China, with its decline and then rise in the economic market, displays its persevering desire for economic growth. It still aims to move forward in the social, economic, and political race. This perseverance has given China its current growth. China has become a world leader in solar technology. It has developed cities and raised the standard of living. It has regained its position, as the largest exporter in the world. It has manufactured for foreign companies and holds importance in the business of trade. In addition, China is also the largest foreign holder of U.S. Treasury bills.

Before the onset of the economic reforms of 1978, China was considered a poor country. It may be difficult to digest, but the country shared a GDP per capita similar to that of Zambia. Following the reforms, China's economy took an upturn, with the country's GDP per capita growing almost around 10% every year, till 2014. As the GDP grew,

CHINA

China was able to pull 800 million of its people out of poverty – an achievement, one doesn't get to see that often.

China contributed more than 75% of the total reduction in global poverty, between the years 1990 and 2005. This was majorly achieved through strengthening the country's manufacturing sector that focused on labor-intensive production, creating jobs, and livelihood for its people. It wasn't long before China saw the impact of these economic measures in the form of a growing middle-class population.

With an increase in their disposable incomes, Chinese people culminated into a thriving market for lifestyle products, services, and experiences. The Chinese population is more inclined towards spending on premium products and services, as they move up the income ladder. However, the people largely remain driven by savings, which has made China's progress into becoming a consumption-driven economy slightly sluggish.

There are a couple of other challenges, like the unfavorable climate for agriculture and the rising inflation, but that doesn't hold the Chinese back from progressing forward. However, it's not difficult to face and overcome these challenges, as it is just going to require more years to achieve the growth that China truly desires.

With persistence and its advancement in technology, education, and innovation, China can possibly become a dominating country on the globe. There has been a real estate explosion in the U.S, London, and Australia, etc. This has attracted Chinese buyers to invest in properties. In Australia, Chinese investors are buying assets ranging from housing to port facilities.

Over the past year, Chinese investment in Australia's agricultural sector went from $300 million to more than $1 billion. Similarly, in the U.S., Chinese are the top buyers of homes. According to NAR (National Association of Realtors), they hit the record of being the top buyers of residential property for three straight years, surpassing buyers from the U.K, Mexico, India, and Canada.

Moreover, they have also invested in buying commercial property in London, especially after Britain voted to leave the European Union. They are slowly taking over in terms of economy and business. It is likely that China will make major progress in the coming years, and flourish more and more.

China is an ancient and mysterious land, filled with adventure and discoveries. It has a variety of geographical locations with abundant resources, minerals, animals, and plants which have been preserved over generations. The Chinese people are proud of their historical background, culture, and its unique traditions.

This diversity conjures up interest in people coming from all over the world. Its unique arts and crafts, calligraphy, silk, and embroidery cannot be found anywhere else. Above all, Kung Fu is also well-renowned throughout the world, and is recognized as a Chinese tradition.

Moreover, their cuisine and cultural heritage have reached all corners of the Earth. The food is especially loved all over the world. Overall, China is a nation that is filled with treasures, and it invites people from around the world, to at least come and visit once in a lifetime.

Chapter 3 - Relationships & Credibility

Amidst the rich cultural heritage, technological and global advancements, and the extravagantly diverse lifestyle, China holds an enormous significance for relationships and credibility.

Like any other country, China too has a distinguished place for establishing and maintaining relationships not just within the local people or the foreign immigrants, or between entrepreneurs working together in the business world, but also in having a connective bond across the borders.

The Chinese people thrive off relationships. The importance of relationships in so engraved in the Chinese culture and tradition, that fundamentally everything comprises or somehow relates to establishing relationships and trust. It penetrates into almost every aspect of the core values of the Chinese people: family and friendships, lifestyle, business, government, and foreign alliances.

Overall, China's importance of prizing relationships, even in an age of social disconnect all around the world has successfully entrenched harmony and peace, within the country. Here, relationships and trust are considered more than just metaphors. They flow through the lifestyle of people, and it reflects in their cultural values.

Thus, we will study its importance, its impact on the business world, and how to establish relationships and credibility in China. This will further enhance your knowledge of this beautiful place, and give an insight as to why you must travel to China and gain personal experience.

Importance Of Relationships In China

Relationships are a pivotal facet of Chinese life. Whether it be family relationships, friendships, or business relationships, Chinese people hold trust and affinity in high regard. A Chinese social psychologist Hwang (1986) divided relationships among Chinese people into three categories:

- Affective - relationships with family members and close friends.

- Instrumental - relationships with the parties, one deals with in order to achieve practical ends.
- Mixed or Guanxi - relationships that have both an affective and instrumental dimension.

Let's begin with examining the first type of relationship, i.e. *"affective"* which includes the relationship with family and friends. The family is the primary institution where you learn the most basic values. It plays a vital role in preparing you to go out in the world, and participate in the societal practices and culture.

The clan we are born and brought up in, ingrains most of the early education that we receive, by which core beliefs are formed in us. As we discussed before, Chinese families are very similar to traditional Asian families, which comprise of an extended family.

They value family relationships and you find the people are closely knit together in this bond. You will find that a typical Chinese family will most likely contain parents, their children, and the grandparents. While in other cultures, grandparents may not live along with their children and their grandchildren.

Chinese culture considers this family bond, as a basic ethical requirement. However, there have been many changes in the past, but it has not affected this Chinese way of thinking. Chinese people also believe and remain true for establishing friendships. The importance of friendship in Chinese tradition has also been historic.

The Chinese literati tradition and Confucian role ethics have had deep roots and influence on the Chinese society. The classical philosophy and literary texts also contain stories that illustrate the importance of friendship and family. There are three of the five Confucian cardinal relationships, which are an example of the ideal behavior and harmony.

They are: father-son, husband-wife, and elder brother-younger brother. These relationships fall into the category of *"affective relationships"*, and they are always viewed as bonds that must be prized above all. Friendships in the Chinese society are based on trust. This is largely imperative in the field of business, and it is not astonishing that entrepreneurs emphasize on establishing a companionship with each other first, before commencing the business activities in order to have trust and credibility in their relationships.

Relationships In The Business World

Entrepreneurs all around the world would agree that business is all about building relationships. This notion is widely held and adhered in China. The Chinese word for relationships is "*Guanxi*", but it is treated more like a philosophy. It is believed that having "*guanxi*" makes you fortunate enough to have a stronger network of contacts – connecting with people who are richer.

These contacts, more precisely may be considered as Western companies, as they are rich as well as present the huge market that they belong to. Building this "*Guanxi*" takes time in China. It cannot take place in the matter of days or weeks. In fact, it may require several months or even years to build it.

Moreover, to build it, you have to provide an equal amount of favor, as compared to what you are accepting for your own business. This, as a practice, has taken deep roots in the business world over the course of years. Chinese business culture is rapidly changing, as the country exposes itself to global businesses and organizations. They have grown to emphasize the partnership in business and the accomplishments resulting from them.

Subsequently, adding weightage to the value brought in by a potential partner, and whether they can be trusted and relied upon or not. This has bridged a gap between Western executives and the Chinese entrepreneurs. Foreign and local businesspersons now seek to understand each other's business needs, and have confidence in each other. Consequently, a workable path is created through that mutual understanding based on negotiations and *"sincerity."*

Sincerity, as we all know, is a strengthening factor for personal bonds and when this is incorporated in the field of business, an increasing number of business dealings are carried out, far more effectively than before. Chinese people reflect these sincerities in their business practices. The gestures they make during business interactions include sharing gifts, providing a service free of cost, or giving out sample materials free of charge.

These simple gestures are a great strategy to make the corporate bond stronger as they promote friendliness among people. Many foreign companies have been attracted to this approach, and it has compelled them to enter into fruitful business agreements with their Chinese counterparts.

However, there is a disadvantageous side to this positivity. Westerners may tend to exploit this friendliness and take advantage of it. They may tend to make unreasonable requests, and misuse the trust and generosity of the Chinese businesspersons, but that is not always the case. *"Guanxi"*, therefore, is essential in business but it has to begin with trust and sincerity, and remain in continuum throughout the course of the relationship.

The Chinese culture teaches us that in order to carry out effective business practices, you have to amalgamate the practical and the emotional factors attached to the process. In other cultures, this idea might be viewed as risky and unprofessional for the progress of the company. However, the teachings of the Chinese culture preach otherwise, and these people may not even agree to carry out trade in the absence of trust.

So, if you wish to establish a business in China, you must not forget the importance of sincere relationships and mutual reliability. Developing this interpersonal relationship may take time, as the Chinese businesspersons emphasize needing more time to know and evaluate a certain someone. However, once that trust is established, things are likely to move forward quickly and bestow long-term benefits to both parties involved.

Chinese Relationships Across The Borders

The overall establishment and maintenance of a country's relationships with its neighboring countries are extremely important, to ensure its national security and economic stability. It helps in maintaining peace, which is essential for economic development and a favorable neighborhood environment. Chinese culture has also successfully managed to establish relationships, across the borders. This populous country does not only impart such values within the country or on a regional level; rather, it spreads its cultural traditions globally.

Such beliefs and traditions have played a massive role in making China prosper in all fields, whether it is technology or business. In today's world, no other country has as many neighbors as China. North Korea, Russia, Mongolia,

Kazakhstan, Kyrgyzstan, Tajikistan, Afghanistan, Pakistan, India, Nepal, Bhutan, Myanmar, Laos, and Vietnam surround China. There have been relationships issues with other countries of which a prominent example is Japan.

Although China and Japan are neighboring countries that are separated from each other only by the East China Sea, their relationship has worsened over the years. China has had great influence over the Japanese lifestyle, culture, and philosophy. Yet, their relationship has not been particularly good. This is due to the Japanese government's refusal to give the Chinese people, a much-needed acknowledgment for its wartime atrocities.

This act angered the Chinese politicians and things took a downturn from there. But the two countries continue to trade with each other, even though their foreign relations stay to be a matter of concern for the UN. Despite, having such issues, China has successfully managed to resolve border disputes since the 1990s.

China easily resolved the Central Asian borders by making concessions to enlist the supporting governments, in fighting a perceived security threat. However, to reach an agreement with Russia, it took about a decade. Nevertheless, China has always made its neighboring countries feel like it is not a bully, by using peaceful strategies to maintain the relationships. It had also gained respect from them in this matter. Being such a vast territory, it is clearly difficult for China to establish a good relationship with every country across the border. However, the country has successfully managed to maintain friendly relationships with Pakistan, Kazakhstan, and Laos through agreements over joint development and trade relations. Other countries like the Philippines, Myanmar, Malaysia, Brunei, and Indonesia too have adopted a foreign policy of setting differences with China aside, to achieve mutual benefits.

China is the world's second largest economy after the United States, and its rise and expansion exhibit its abilities in maintaining relationships all around the world. It has wisely used diplomatic approaches and strategies, to extend its influence across the borders.

It is still working ambitiously towards revitalizing the ancient Chinese civilization and we will see in the upcoming years, how China approaches its neighbors to reach these global ambitions.

Establishing Relationships and Credibility

A Chinese executive at Google said, *"In China, your success depends on how well a person trusts you."* This is essential to understand, if you want to visit China or establish relationships with the Chinese people for friendships or for business relationships. The heart of any successful long-term relationship, especially cross-cultural business relationships, is trust. Trust removes all room for doubt and disappointment when it comes to businesses.

As westerners or foreign immigrants, you will have to learn to develop this trust over time, to help in business dealings. When this trust, or as earlier studied *"Guanxi"* is established, you can easily resolve difficult issues, share ideas and strategies, and work collectively with the Chinese. Therefore, to develop these interpersonal relationships, the key is to build cognitive and affective trust.

To begin with, it is essential to understand your own

mental capabilities, your background, and how you are going to deal with these cultural issues, when visiting China. It is likely that you have already formed an image in your mind. These are cultural assumptions that have rooted in stereotypes. These assumptions can really interfere when you are attempting to establish foreign relationships, and will stop you from being cooperative towards them. It will keep you from building a rapport, and your communication will generally lack connectivity. Therefore, if you desire to establish your relationships with the Chinese, you have to use the right skills. You need to be mindful of your assumptions and interpretation of the Chinese culture and tradition.

As a foreigner, your assumptions may not be accurate enough and sticking to your own mindset may cause a lot of misunderstanding, before you even start to establish relationships. To deal with this, you can just observe the people and check your assumptions against that. While there are global differences in culture and tradition, you may also find cultural differences in different provinces, regions, and business norms within the country.

Therefore, you have to abandon the already ingrained beliefs, and be open to learning and experiencing these new and unique differences. It may be a little difficult, but the advice of a local, cultural guide can always prove to be helpful in your journey. Language can play a huge part in mingling with people and making friends. It can serve to be a powerful tool for cultural navigation and it is, therefore, equally important when you come to China. Learning Chinese or Mandarin can enable you to have one-to-one conversations without the involvement of a translator, thereby further diminishing the possibilities of misunderstandings and misconceptions. This is the reason why many westerners have now started to invest time in learning these languages to remove the barrier, and connect more freely and effectively with Chinese people.

However, even though the language is immensely significant, it still is not a substitute for cultural knowledge. A Chinese managing partner for a global recruitment firm said, *"Even though people may not understand each other's language, they can still communicate well. It's all about understanding each other's culture."*

Therefore, having knowledge of the Chinese culture, traditional values, and norms remains the source of establishing relationships and credibility. To gain this cultural knowledge, you can spend more time with them, understand their families, their experiences, their backgrounds, their customs, and etiquettes. This will enable you to look at their lifestyles more closely, and learn what pleases and displeases them.

You will be able to build a personal dimension and gain the awareness of their culture and traditions, which will help you in developing strong relationships. The same approach could be applied to business relationships, in addition. As Chinese people value their personal sentiments and emotions even in professional activities, unlike the western business relationships where a personal connection is secondary.

Overall, establishing relationships and credibility in China is completely dependent on trust, understanding, and sincerity; and the more you learn the Chinese culture, the more you will appreciate the beauty of it.

Traveling To China For Business

China is extremely exotic and dynamic in its material culture. To truly dive into this culture and make new experiences, you must travel to China to see, feel, touch, and taste this country. Its profound history, art, and material culture is embodied in everything and is highly influenced by Buddhism. Their temples are surely a sight to visit, in order to feast your eyes on high public art and architecture.

The clay statues, iron flagpoles, and bronze bells in the temple buildings display the craft skills of the local people, and how the early Chinese empire was integrated with them. Its vast territory is also rich in picturesque landscapes and stands out, as one of the most beautiful natural sceneries. China has several multihued mountains like *"Rainbow Mountains"* located in The Danxia Landscape in Zhangye, *"The Yellow Mountains"* located in Huangshan in all their mysticism, the precipitous pillars in Zhangjiajie, which are famous for its rock pillars and deep valleys, the *Yuangyang* terraced fields, the *Li River, Yangshuo*, and many other magnificent sights that are great attractions.

All this makes China a place worth visiting – even if it's just for business. Therefore, if you are traveling for business purposes, mingling with the Chinese people, and trying to integrate into their culture and traditions is going to assist you, in building the *"Guanxi"* needed for a successful business. However, it is essential for you to understand that the Chinese already have a difficult time trusting people when making business deals with them, even within their own country.

This makes it all the more difficult for the people coming from a foreign land to do business with them. So, when you enter into this land, make sure you interact with them, take part in their practices, and adapt to their values and etiquettes. Allow yourself to submerge in their traditions and make new learning experiences, by actively engaging with them. The Chinese are impressed when they find their culture being appreciated. They feel honored and respected, thereby feel more drawn to establish business relationships on the basis of closeness, rapport, and empathy.

Like we mentioned before, Chinese people take time in coming to a business agreement with an entrepreneur. They prefer to invest their time in evaluating and getting to know their business contacts on a personal level. Hence, when you travel to China on a business venture, make sure you are mindful of their culture, values, and norms.

Let the knowledge from your experiences in China sink in, and build the bridges between you and your Chinese counterparts. This will enable you to connect with them on a personal level and through this personal dimension, establish a successful cross-cultural business relationship.

Ways To Build Relationships In China

As we know that the sale starts with the relationship, not the product, it is important to study the ways to build relationships:

Build A Network

Building a network is the basic concept of *Guanxi*. It involves friends, family, business associates, and government officials. You have to make sure you reciprocate the favors and treatment that you are given by them. It should not be one-sided but should be equal from both ends, so that a stronger relationship is established.

The Concept Of Face

Face is a sociological concept that involves respect, honor, and reputation. It is something that can be earned and lost, and it holds a deeper significance within the Chinese community. In China, when your face is lost, it is hard to regain it unlike in the US. When a politician or celebrity loses face in the US, they may be forgiven but not in China. Therefore, the maintenance of face is vital in creating relationships with people.

Study Language And Culture

Another way to build relationships is by learning Mandarin. Learning the language of any country, removes a few communicational barriers, and makes it easier to learn their culture and mix with them. Even some knowledge of the language can help a lot. Learning phrases in their tongue can impress your Chinese friends, colleagues, and business partners; and can show them that you are open-heartedly accepting their culture, and are willing to establish *Guanxi*.

Go For Dinners And Eat The Food They Make

Food is a means that not only connects people on one table but channels a way for interaction between them. Accepting dinner invites and having dinner with your friends and colleagues and even business partners, will help you know them better. You can try new dishes and don't forget to compliment them. This will display your ability to mingle and be open to new things.

Navigate Business Holidays

Make use of holidays such as Chinese New Year. Participating in such events and festivals is another way to interact with people, besides formal situations. Moreover, holidays are a way to free yourself from work. Therefore, meeting in these times is a sign that you want to interact with people and know them personally, even on days when you are not obliged to.

Chapter 4 - Where You Sit Matters

Any society that exists in this world has a culture of its own. This culture is the life and blood of a civilization without which it cannot uphold its vibrancy, originality and distinct individuality. The culture itself is the society's creative expression of telling people how that specific region leads their lives, and what values they hold. It helps people form a distinguished identity, and shapes the perceptions of foreigners regarding its intrinsic value.

Besides being a reflection of its own identity, it also molds the identity of the people who are born in that culture, and then grew up watching those traditions unfold in front of them. Therefore, to separate culture from a society is absolutely insane, as it snatches the true essence of it.

The era that we live in has made distances smaller, and exposed us all to each other's' traditions. This has given people a way to adopt things that they like in different ethnicities, and making it their own. This concept has given the chance to adopt a uniformity in everything that we do.

There are numerous examples of countries that have gradually eliminated the importance of culture from their society, and have chosen to be modernized. Yet, there are some countries that have knitted themselves with their ancient culture and tradition. In this chapter, we will study the importance of culture, not just for a country but also for a business. We will also look upon the several differences in the cultures of China and America in detail. The two countries are very different from each other, in almost every regard. Geographically, America is in the West, while China is in the East.

There are people residing in America from all around the world, but in China, the number of immigrants is not as much. American people have migrated to this land from somewhere else, but Chinese people have been living in their country for thousands of years. In order to understand the cultural differences of these two countries, let us first have a look at the cultural history of these two countries, so that we may have a better understanding about how their cultures came into being.

CHINA

Chinese culture is thousands of years old and the people of the country hold it in high regards. In the previous chapter, we have already established the importance of relationships and credibility for the Chinese people. This is because these people do not take their traditions lightly, they respect their traditions and elders, and believe that their life experiences will only lead them to success. Respect is one of the fundamental aspects of Chinese society, and they believe in respecting others, especially their elders.

Apart from respect, etiquettes are also an important part of Chinese culture. Collectivism is a very important element of Chinese society. They believe that everything they do is not their achievement, but the achievement of a whole group, or family, or team, or company. They believe that success is something that you can achieve, only with a group of people and not individually.

They believe in bringing everyone together and moving forward, without leaving anyone behind. Chinese also treat their guests with great respect, so much so that they even reserve special places for their guests to sit. Even if their guests are their friends, they would still formally welcome them and have dinner with them, showing them that they are important to the hosts.

The culture of the United States of America, on the other hand, originates from Western (European) culture, but it has become a mixture of different societies. The US is a place where lots of people from around the world have migrated in order to start new lives. This has led the country into accepting people from different cultures and to some extent, accept some parts of their cultures and make them their own. American soil has been ruled by many countries over the years, before America's Independence.

The rule of these countries in America has left its trait in the American culture. America, as we know it now, has been colonized by Spain, France, Russia, Denmark, and many other countries. Cultural influences in America have been brought in by Germany, Japan, Italy, and Ireland. Immigration has also brought different cultures to the country, for example, the Latin American culture, African-American culture, and Asian American culture.

We can clearly see that the history of these two countries is very different from one another. Chinese people have lived in China for thousands of years, while American people, as they are called in today's world, have taken over the land in the past centuries, and have merged different cultures to make a new American culture. The differences in the history of these two countries have created societies with different thinking processes. The Chinese people are more influenced by their ancestors, their traditions, and culture; while in comparison, the American people are more influenced by people from different parts of the world. In this aspect, the culture of China is more traditional than it is in America.

Privacy

The concept of privacy is very different in China and America. The American people think that things like marital status, income, and age is something private, and they are not very open in discussing such things and telling about themselves. They believe in the concept of privacy, i.e. it does not really matter what a person does in his/her personal life, as long as it does not affect his/her professional life. Personal and professional lives are different in America.

They are more concerned about their privacy in

comparison to the Chinese people, as long as it concerns their private life. American people give more liberty to their children, so much in fact, that they let their children go after eighteen years of age to make their own lives. After graduating from college in America, young adults find jobs and move out of their parents' house to live their own life. Chinese people are more traditional, as we have already discussed, and it may even seem that they do not give as much liberty to their children. But the fact of the matter is, that they give more importance to their cultural and family values. Even in a group of people, it is more important to think about the benefit of the group as a whole, than to think of one's own self-interest.

Chinese believe working together with trust is the right way to success. Americans, being members of a capitalist society, believe in a person's own self-interest more than anything else. They believe that if every person in their society thinks only about their own self-interest, then the whole society will flourish on its own, because everyone will be thinking of themselves. So, they will succeed, and so will the whole society.

They believe that the best way of getting a person to do something, is to merge their own self-interest with it, so they will be internally motivated to successfully complete the task. Chinese people think highly of their mentors and elders, and would gladly place their own interest after the interest of their elders. Instead of self-interest, they use their values as motivators. Children in China will work to make their parents proud, and make a name for their family. They believe in themselves but will try harder to achieve a task successfully, if the honor of their family is on the line. Americans do not give that much importance to their family names, instead, they believe only in themselves.

Family

Family and honor are very important for the Chinese. They are more traditional, so they give more importance to the elders of their society. Young people in China treat their elders with dignity and respect, and in return, they are nurtured and cherished. Americans promote self-interest to make people do their jobs, but Chinese promote the honor of their family. Children in China are more pampered, in comparison to the children in America.

Chinese give more time and thought about the way in which they will manage the upbringing of their children.

And they make sure that their child stays on track, by giving them enough time and going along with them on every step of the way. The importance of family for Chinese people can be understood by thinking about the difference between a house and a home.

For a lot of people these two words may be interchangeable, but for Chinese people, these two words are very different from one another. Chinese believe that a house can be any building, but it can only become a home if you have emotional attachment and ties with that building; for example, family members living in the same house, memories with the family members, and good and bad times spent together.

Americans do not give as much importance to their families, they believe that their parents are there, only to help guide them until they are of legal age, i.e. eighteen years of age. After that, they are free to do whatever they want with their lives. The parents also do not expect their children to hang around, to take care of them. They let their children go so that they may make the most from their lives, without having anything to hold them back from success. Americans believe a lot more in independence, than keeping their family together.

They believe that families only hold their children back if they expect their children to take care of parents in their old age; the Chinese, on the other hand, believe that they will never succeed without the help of their family, and even if they do succeed, it will not be as honorable as taking care of their family. Chinese believe that success will eventually come their way, if they stay strong as a family. Such independent behavior in America, leads the elderly to live lonely lives only with their spouses, if they stay married until they get old. Their children may come to visit them every six months in the beginning, if their relationship had been healthy in their childhood. Otherwise, they may not even visit their parents in years. Elderly people in China live with their families mostly until they die, they live not only with their children but also with their grandchildren when they are born

Friends

The concept of friends and friendship are also very different in the American and Chinese cultures. Chinese people do not call just anyone they meet their friends.

Friendship in Chinese culture has more importance in a person's life, than it has in the American culture. When a Chinese becomes friends with you, he/she remains your friend until their last breath, as long as there is trust. A Chinese person will go out of their way to help their friend. They will introduce them to their family members, and from that point onwards, both the families will know each other. Friendship in America is very different in many ways. People in America will call anyone as their friends, if they have talked to each other at least once. Americans, in general, will call anyone their friends when they meet them, and they have friends for different things, such as in work they will have work friends; if they play games together, they will have playing friends; and they have school friends; and even friends who drink together. Americans may have different friends for different life aspects, but the Chinese have only a few but very good friends, who will help them out if they are in need.

Americans may think that friendship in the Chinese culture is more of a practical thing than emotional, but the same is not true. This difference in thinking stems from the different mindsets of people in the two cultures. For Americans, friendship is very informal; while for Chinese, it can be very formal. The difference is because there is not much value given to etiquettes in the American culture. Chinese people are not very direct, even if they do not like something about their friend, they might not say it directly so that it would not hurt that person's feelings. American friendship is very informal, they might call their friends 'shorty', or 'fatty', just for its fun, but Chinese people would never make fun of their friends like that. Chinese are traditional, which is why they appreciate when someone gives them gifts or asks them to come over for dinners. In giving these gifts and asking to come over for dinner, the gift itself or the dinner itself is not as important for the Chinese people, as is the thought of giving a gift or asking someone to come over for dinner.

They do not see the monetary value of the gift or dinner, but rather the thought process that was behind it. This is the way Chinese friendships grow stronger, but in view of Americans it might be labeled as 'buying friendship'. One cannot outrightly say that Chinese friendship is better than American or vice versa, what is more important is to understand the cultural differences, and accepting both types of friendships.

Money

People of Chinese and American cultures think differently about money as well. Chinese people do not spend with an open hand, as they like to save more. They save money for emergencies and for any special occasion that may not be a part of their current planning. Chinese are wise to think like that, because it is always better to save money for unplanned situations than to rely on someone else. Americans do not believe in the concept of saving money. They buy almost everything on credit and start paying off, after 2 or more years in installments.

The system in America is such that the government takes care of all the medical needs of families, so that they will not need to spend their hard-earned money for medical reasons. They just save enough so that they may be able to go on vacations, from time to time and to some extent, to pay off the college fees for their children.

Education

A person might say that America has some of the best universities in the world, but this does not mean that the culture of the country gives more importance to education.

CHINA

In China, people give a lot of value to education and career. Chinese people make sure that their children are well taken care of, in schools as well as in homes. They make sure that they teach their children the things that they are not learning in schools or colleges.

One of the most important things the Chinese learn from their families is the importance of family, tradition, and culture. They teach their children that it is far more important for a person to be loyal to his/her family than anything else. Such thinking does not normally contradict with learning or studying in schools, as being loyal to your family means that you have to make your family proud by successfully completing your education, and making a difference in the world after starting a job.

Parents in China, do not let their children enjoy their leisure time all the time, they instill the importance of education and career in their children, and divide the time so that their child might enjoy but only for a limited period of time, and would utilize the rest of the time in learning and practicing for their schools or careers.

Americans think differently about education. Most people in America only to study till colleges and only a few complete universities They believe that a person's good character and faith can lead them to succeed in life. This thinking of the American people may have stemmed from the diverse cultures that exist in the country.

Unlike China, where everyone is from the same culture and have almost the same values, in America people from all kinds of backgrounds and cultures have come together to live, their children going to schools together. This communication with people from other cultures makes a person think whether they are doing right by following what they believe or if the other person's beliefs are better. This leads to thinking and accepting elements from other cultures, which might not always be good, causing the declining importance of education in America.

CHINA

Chapter 5 – Trust

When it comes to Chinese people, trust is one of the most important elements when forming a productive relationship. The same thing applies to when doing business with them, in fact, to a much greater degree. However, it is important to understand that Chinese people and their culture only allow one to be a business partner or a friend.

The Chinese culture does not allow them to build two relationships at a time. So either you play the role of a business partner or the role of a friend, but never both together. If trust is ever lost in either relationship, you will never be able to regain it when it comes to the Chinese.

Creating that element of trust between yourself and the Chinese is a daunting task. Unlike the Western culture, where trust is gained by offering others the benefit of the doubt, Chinese culture is entirely opposite. With Chinese people, you have to earn the trust first. This way of thinking stems from a deeply rooted culture from which the Chinese people belong.

CHINA

A culture based on religious sentiments and core values, the Chinese are known to establish relationships and value them in the highest accord. Each relationship they have, whether as a parent, son/daughter, friend, and even a business partner will have a different connotation and therefore, will be treated accordingly. China is one of the largest economies in the world and is currently standing as the second largest economy, right behind the United States of America.

Truth is that the way things are shaping out to be, it would not be long before China surpasses the United States of America, probably in the next ten years. This shift of power makes it more than necessary to not only understand how Chinese culture and values work in accordance with business ties, but to also understand the dos and don'ts with Chinese business partners.

However, such relationships do not come this easily. The Chinese work differently as compared to Western people. Therefore, regardless of whether you have formed a business or a friendly relationship, it is important to understand the Chinese culture and work style. It is necessary to do this because if you are planning to invest your time for future endeavors, it would be easy to construct a plan.

We all are self-aware of what trust is about, and to a lot of us, it is a very important tool to run a successful business. We think that we should trust implicitly. In China, however, this is not the case. Trust is something that the Chinese hold to be very expensive, and by that what I mean is that trust in China is not given away immediately unlike in other countries, especially in the west.

Trust in China is not given quickly and not taken away quickly either – the complete opposite of what happens in the Western World. A famous Chinese fable, where a man took his grandson to one of his old childhood friend's home. Upon seeing his friend, the child was in awe of him and hid himself by sheltering his body behind his grandfather.

Shocked by his grandson's behavior, who was usually friendly and talkative, the grandfather asked his friend to gift an apple to his grandson from a nearby bowl. Upon this gesture, the child quickly familiarized himself with his grandfather's friend and immediately started a conversation, as if they were friends from long before.

Surprised by this act, the old friend asked the grandfather as to why the kid had suddenly changed his behavior towards him. The grandfather simply replied saying that for kids, reputation does not matter. What matters is the fact to build trust. It is important to provide the other with a positive gesture just like you did, by offering the apple.

Thus, courtesy demands reciprocity and only then can a real relationship grow. This fable should be understood from a much larger context and one that confronts many Western firms that are wishing to establish business relationships with China. They must build a system of trust first, when there is barely any foundation for a relationship.

What is more concerning to them is the fact that by Western definitions and culture, the meaning of trust differs largely from what trust means back in China or how it is applied. From what can be understood from the fable, a strong and deeply rooted relationship based on a positive gesture is a prerequisite, for one to have a successful relationship with any Chinese businessman or firm.

What Trust Means In China

Although, many Western firms and business are of the understanding that the rules of Chinese interpersonal relationships are very complicated, and that they always lead towards nepotism, deception, and corruption. While this just might be a big misunderstanding and comes from a difference of culture, it shows a bigger disregard towards Chinese culture and ignorance towards it. The west has, for far too long ignored the nuances of the relationship development in China.

For the west, by default, trust is something that is already guaranteed when starting either a friendship, a business relationship, or even a mere tinder date. In the west, it is all about giving the benefit of the doubt and that the other shall trust you, until you indulge yourself in an act where you break the other's trust. However, in China things are different and by default, it not trust but rather *"distrust"*.

You will only be trusted once you have proven yourself worthy of being trusted. Just as in the case of the fable, the kid had started trusting his grandfather's friend, only after a positive gesture was offered. This behavior is portrayed in a more eloquent manner through a famous Chinese saying which is *"Early birds get shot"* (qiang da Chu tou niao) – which is all about avoiding social risks and being hurt. While in America, such an attitude is possibly looked down upon or is considered too cautious. In China, if you are able to achieve the building of trust of another, only then can you do business. However, in the west – people are accustomed to doing business, regardless of the trust factor being there and people start doing business together almost immediately.

The west is more comfortable with conducting business and building trust, all at the same time – if the opportunity is there. American Executives are known to make strong distinctions between trusting someone based on their professional competence, and trusting someone based on their relationship with them. While for Chinese executives, both types of trust are required.

This difference clearly indicates the need for an interpersonal trust relationship to be cemented, before one starts conducting business in China or with the Chinese. To understand, why the Chinese chose to behave in such a manner, we must consider how people from different cultures and especially China, define the initial function of trust. In China, the main function of trust it to protect and establish feelings of safety.

While in the west, it has more to do with exploring and establishing where there can be a future possibility of a fertile ground of opportunities. We can take this argument and back it up with a very clichéd thought of the west, continuously exploring the idea of a blind date. A blind date, is one where the future can hold endless possibilities, and both parties are willing to explore.

While the west has more to do with being all about an individualistic culture, where people acquire skills for themselves, to form alliances and a network to survive. Therefore, a person hailing from a Western culture will take a more active approach towards building a relationship and by default, trusting the other person without having any prior knowledge about them.

On the contrary, people from China are quite the opposite. Not being an individualistic nature, the Chinese people hail from a more relational culture and not a collectivistic culture, as wrongly accused of being one. A relational culture, where *"Guanxi"* is a Chinese concept that refers to a tight form of social network, which forms the Chinese society as a whole. People in the same *Guanxi* will have an automatic trust between them, but it will never be assumed outside of it.

Therefore, distrust by default is a Chinese norm. Only when one is sure that a new relationship that is being formed will have no side effects or any threat (but will rather preserve), only then will trust be given. With all that is going on with the Chinese economy and how it is progressing, the world should agree that at some point building a strong relationship with the Chinese is important, especially in business terminology.

Therefore, it is imperative to understand the way Chinese people operate, especially with regards to their business activities. Therefore, it is clear that when dealing with the Chinese, you will have to earn trust beforehand, before you wish to proceed with having business terms with them.

How Can People Outside The Chinese Society Form A Relationship Based On Trust With The Chinese?

The Chinese dominance that they have over the world economy should only be respected and admired. Therefore, how can you – from a Western point of you, approach the Chinese in a business situation, when it is all about forming an alliance based on trust initially?

Understandably, it takes time to develop a relationship especially one based on trust. The Chinese businessmen are known to invest a decent amount of time and effort, in getting to know you in person. On the contrary, a person from a Western dialect may already be discussing business deals that the Chinese may not even be thinking or have on his mind, because they will still be in the phase of evaluating you.

While this may seem to be quite frustrating, as the business during this passage of time may be going nowhere – but one must consider and understand that things will go a lot faster and smoother once trust is achieved, especially from the Chinese end towards you – the Western people. If your business deals are still in place and in the initial stages and no personal relationship exists as of yet with the Chinese – be aware of trying to build trust through social means, as there is a good chance it might backfire.

Giving the Chinese people gifts, organizing social events, and parties in their honor, there is a strong possibility that it can work against you. Because your Chinese counterparts are still in the evaluating phase – you have to make sure, that all your steps are well calculated because you're being thoroughly judged. During the initial stages, it is important that you concern your possible Chinese business partners with your competence and expertise, rather than just simply talking about it or charming them through it. Neither will they give into these social gathering or gifts, but in fact, it will all go against you. Your main concern should be in making sure, that the Chinese understand that you are more concerned about getting the job done, and that you care as much as them about the business you are to venture into.

Also important to understand is that when building and nurturing a business relationship, you might also be asked some personal questions or even be asked to share stories, especially ones which contain information of a personal nature with your contacts. This is only done by the Chinese to get to know you better, and people from the west might consider this to be something creepy and of an awkward nature, but this is how it's done.

The Chinese are very concerned about getting to know you better, and this is one of their ways to do it. You may even be asked about how much money you make, or about your religious beliefs. It is all about building a relationship, which is an essential part of their cultural etiquette, and doing business in China or with people from China.

Once you have passed the initial stage, and a business relationship is established, which by default means that the Chinese have started trusting you as you are already in the working phase with them, make sure that you hold on to that trust; and not just holding on to it, but rather building on that foundation. For it is important for your Chinese counterpart to understand and feel that through this business deal, a sense of benevolence exists – which will be good for the business in the long term.

One should understand and keep in mind that building trust and achieving it with the Chinese is strenuous and also very time consuming, but the level of trust that can be achieved can last forever. As the Chinese say *"once a promise is made, it cannot be withdrawn, not even with the forces of four horse powers."*

It has been universally recognized that Chinese business environment is different than any other business environment in the world. The key difference lies in *guanxi*. Business people, from both China and Western countries, approach a new relationship from opposite ends altogether. A small example would be Commercial Law, which is an important element of Western thinking and other parts of the world, is completely ignored in the Chinese business environment and barely exists there. According to Chinese people, commercial law indicates bad faith and the business clauses at the most form a functional agenda. While Western people include commercial law to assure others that business deals being approached will be honored and therefore, will be placed. For the Chinese people, this indicates a fragile relationship between two parties and that legal sanctions are needed to bind their words together.

This is not appreciated amongst the Chinese. However, recently; the Chinese authorities have initiated the use of commercial laws, but only to accommodate Western expectations and people. A few businessmen are yet to rely on it entirely.

You Are Either A Friend Or A Business Partner But Never Both

However, when it comes to the Chinese, you can either be a business partner or a friend to them. There exists no in-between with them. The Chinese people hold their values strictly, and are very serious about their work. Not taking away anything from the Western people, but the Chinese at the time of doing business, will only think about doing business and its future, nothing else. While trust is an important factor before business deals are signed, friendship is also held with high regard. As the importance of a business deal to them is already told, friendship is also held with the same regard, and they can never be mingled together. The Chinese often go to great lengths in relationship building to open doors for those within their social network, and trust them to a degree that would surprise many from the west.

As the famous Chinese saying goes *"Gold is easy to get, a close friend is harder to find."* This saying reveals the attitude Chinese people have towards friendship – as they appreciate it and believe in it thoroughly. Chinese people value good friends and if made once, it can last a lifetime. Also, the Chinese people will, therefore, never mingle friendships with their business which is why, you will barely see a Chinese initiating a business with one of their friends.

In fact, the Chinese will never risk their friendships by starting a business together. They understand, business deals are complicated and take time. For them, forming a relationship based on trust and then the business, can go forward but that is about it. There are no strings attached in regards to friendship. The Chinese are known to have strict values, and for them – being friends is as important as anything which is why, they will do nothing to risk their friendship with anyone. For the Chinese, relationships are everything. Each relationship for them holds great value, and is kept in a different setting. They will have rules for all of them, just as with friends, a business partner, wife, and husband etc. It is important to understand building relationships with your partners that are open to new ideas and a fresh way of thinking, regardless of whether they are agents, distributors, or other partners.

But as the Chinese have understood from long ago, such

alliances come with certain risks and which is why they do not risk it, by becoming friends which simply stems from the value of friends to them; which is held in a much higher degree, as compared to people from the west. For the Chinese, everything that they do, is oriented from values which are inherited from family ages ago, and through those values – business partners are considered different from friends. Friends are considered seriously to be there for a lifetime, and they shall never risk their friendship by doing business with them.

Chapter 6 - The Great Wall of China

In recent years, China has earned a reputation over the world, due to its vast economy and incredible change in social affairs. However, there was a time when *'Hukou'* took place. The Hukou system was introduced by the Communist party of China. Basically, it is a kind of passport system that limits access of local Chinese people to a number of public services, based on the territory and area they belong to.

The Chinese had restrictions to move freely within their own country, and to travel abroad. They had to obtain several permits to do so. Each citizen was classified as agricultural or non-agricultural Hukou, easily referring to as rural or urban citizen respectively. This passport was linked to several benefits.

The government also controlled even internal migration within the city. The Government was quite strict about their citizens. This system was then loosened after the death of Chairman Mao. Mao Zedong was an extraordinary planner, a great writer, and a poet whose vision for China had no boundaries. He had a vision for the country to prosper. After the death of Mao, the former Chairman of the Communist Party of China in 1976, the country's policies slowly began to change. Young Chinese citizens who had been sent to the countryside during the Cultural Revolution, gradually traveled back to the city. They then began to contribute their share of hard work for the country. China's economy slowly began to boost which helped attract millions of other migrants, to move to urban areas, and become low-wage laborers.

The Chinese government always had a focus on providing high-class education to its citizens. This made the Chinese people amongst the first to establish and ritualize good education for its population. In the early 1980s, new leaders of China started building an education system that strongly focused on Math, Science, and the English language. Ever since, the Chinese have been educated to compete with the rest of the world. China currently has a literacy rate of 96.4% measured in the year, 2015.

The education policy in China included building new colleges and universities that helped increase the number of graduates around the country. By the end of 1998, there were 1,022 universities and colleges all around China, 962 adult learning institutions, and 17,106 secondary and technical schools. This boosted the education system in the country within a short period of time. Some rich Chinese people moved out to foreign countries. They took part in Western culture, learned their language skills, and earned their degrees in business subjects. These Chinese residents of the United States, Hong Kong, Malaysia, Macau, Philippines, Singapore, Taiwan, and Thailand flew back to their countries. They then used their learned talents, and invested their earned money and education into their country, to help modernize and globalize the business sector of China.

Chinese people were known for one of their habits. They have always been very humble and very ambitious. They respect even the tiniest matters that we would never think of. Their respect for education and their country leads them to be who they are, and makes them leave a mark wherever they go. The citizens of China treat their country as their home and they believe in it literally.

These Chinese did not stop at only building themselves or their country locally, in fact, they have taken up different initials and measures to earn a name and mark for themselves globally. The Chinese are well known for their modest nature and possess hard working assets. How did the Chinese reach to where they are today? Their habits and upbringing have led China to succeed in different fields.

Education

China's education system is the largest in the world. The Chinese have a strict education system, which is recognized all over the world. Did you know that only 2% of the American 15-year-olds and 3% of the 15-year-old Europeans reach the highest level of Math, whereas, in Shanghai, 30% of the kids in school reach the highest level of Math? That's one difficult level to beat.

China's education credit can be handed out to its teachers. China has a consistent teacher development system in which teachers are assessed and evaluated on a monthly basis, and training and corrections are provided accordingly. Teaching has been, is still, and will remain the most respected profession in China. Teachers hired are well qualified and have acquired vast knowledge to further pass it on to the future generations.

How about the government? The Government of China

has been very beneficent towards its citizens. It has developed the country in many different sectors.

Government

The government has provided China with great education, 90% home ownership, doubling of wages every decade, 80% trust, and 90% approval. No government on earth has reached this level. And I doubt that it could be beaten. The government has played its role in developing the country in different possible ways. It has invested in diverse fields that no other government can think of.

Super Computing

China has invested in the making of the fastest computers in the world. The surprising fact is that China uses only local components. It does not use products manufactured in other countries. These supercomputers are completely made in China. They are among the top 10 of the most energy efficient computers in the world. Now focusing outside this world, China has spread its wings even in outer space. It has also invested in creating satellites to be sent in outer space.

Space

China is now capable of in-space refueling of orbital satellites. There are service satellites that are capable of refueling satellites in space, while they are in action. Similar to air refueling for planes, the process refuels a satellite in orbit, to extend its functional life and boost its capabilities.

Power Generation

China still has vast deposits of coal. It has therefore taken initiatives and used it wisely. China is currently working on nuclear power that will also help them take the lead in the world.

Genomics

America has fallen behind China when it comes to genomic research. The world's largest genome research project of 10,000 people has been launched in China. This will help document their genetic makeup study, to help generate better medicines in the future. The genomic study will enhance the field of pharmaceutics in China. It will also help treat patients better.

Passive Array Radar

China has seven ultra-high-voltage (UHV) production lines of passive array radar in operation, which is more than any other country. It is also leading the line in the development of Metamaterials. These are defined as materials specifically engineered to have properties that have not yet been found in nature. This scientific process helps create materials with such properties in an artificial manner. This new trend is developing in the fields of aerospace and telecommunications.

Thermal Power Generation

China is leading the world by investing in clean energy infrastructure, while still using thermal energy sources. Their thermal power facilities convert coal, oil, and natural gas into electrical energy. Since China is embellished with coal, they take full advantage of it and produce cheap energy which helps the government to provide easily useable to the citizens.

Quantum Communication Networks

China is also becoming the leader in quantum communication technology. Quantum Communication is a satellite that delivers quantum communications, for translating research into strategic assets for Chinese power globally. China is focusing its works on research to further use it for strategic planning to spread Chinese power around the world.

High Speed Trains

Let's not forget that China has the fastest traveling train in the world. It has the capability of traveling up to 20,000 km long routes while carrying 3 million people daily, at the blistering speed of 300 km/h. It was built to help Chinese citizens and ease their mode of traveling within the city.

Radio Telescopy

China has built the largest telescope dish. It measures up to half a kilometer in diameter. It has a 500-meter wide Aperture Spherical Radio, which is equal to around 30 football fields. This telescope dish was under construction since 2011.

This will help search for gravitational waves, new galaxies, and origins of life on other planets. It will be used for communication to other planets for signs of life, if possible. China's rapid growth has accelerated important existing structural trends in the world economy. China has ensured that this will be the era of the global economies. In my opinion, China is bound to succeed in technology and leadership. A country which is focused as well as culture oriented is bound to succeed in all sectors possible.

Brand Success

We are all aware of how rich the Chinese culture is. And comparing it with any other culture is completely absurd; however, it still has not overcome the Western culture in terms of material advancement. Students educated from foreign countries could not get over the Western culture, even after moving back to China. Even residents of foreign countries have moved back to China, but they still brought some of the Western culture with them. This has been the reason that the Western business culture started emerging in China as well.

Top American brand names like Apple, Starbucks, and Procter & Gamble have been dominating the global market for so many years. These brands have also taken over the Chinese market. Chinese people who have spent their life or a part of their life abroad have gained knowledge about these brands. This has given a good opportunity for American companies to enjoy a boost in the Chinese market.

A number of different brands have flourished in China for the past years. These include Intel, Coca-Cola, Gillette, KFC, Microsoft Windows, Nike, and General Motors etc. However, American brands are now facing a threat to their business. According to research carried out recently, local brands have earned about three-quarters of China's market profit in the FMCG industry only, in the previous years.

The recent data shows that US products like Pampers,

Colgate, and Mead Johnson have had a market share drop of 10% in the past five years. This data is based on 40,000 households which mean that 40,000 households have switched from American brands to local brands. Who says China can't build brands? Chinese brands like Haier, HiSense, Air China, Xiaomi, and Lenovo can be seen making their way to the top, amongst international brands.

The dominance of American brands is now threatened, all thanks to the Chinese companies. The Chinese market has put these international brands to shame in some instances. Their market has emerged and taken the world by surprise. Apple's renowned iPhone is known to always make huge sales in China and around the world for quite a long time. However, new data shows that local brands like Oppo, Vivo and the well-established Huawei have put iPhone on the back burner. Huawei has now emerged as the top earning technology brand, and has pushed Apple to number two.

Starbucks, who earned quite a fan following in China has lost sales and reached a low level, due to the local coffee brands. The Chinese people are now also opting for local brands over the international ones. Chinese brands have begun working on creating the same taste of coffee, but at the lowest price possible. This is not only feasible to Chinese citizens, but even to the Government.

China's auto market has also made their way up the list. They are now challenging automobile brands like Ford, General Motors, and the electric carmaker Tesla. Their cars are manufactured locally, and cost less when compared to international cars. Their local cars have the same features of international brands but at a fraction of their cost. Chinese brands are growing and taking over international brands including the high-tech sectors. China is pushing its domestic champions in pharmaceuticals and semiconductors to reduce reliance on international brands. Citizens of China now prefer local brands, and even local medicines for cure. Many brands have even begun their manufacturing process in China. Brands like L.L.Bean, Levis, Radio Flyer, Melissa & Doug Toys, American Girl Dolls, Chuck Taylor, iPhones & iPads, Ray-Ban, and PlayDoh, etc. have part of their manufacturing done in different parts of China.

This manufacturing plan has helped boost the economy by providing jobs to the locals in the country. Foreign investment has also affected the economy of China positively. A decade ago, the Chinese would prefer international brands due to their quality and status. The brand image created in the minds of the Chinese, urged them to pick the international brands over the local ones.

However, things now are quite different. Chinese customers are still conscious of the quality of their purchase. They seek good quality and good service to satisfy their desires, rather than just satisfying their needs. With this knowledge in mind, they are willing to pay more for premium products. Chinese brands are now doing a better job, than they did a decade ago. They have improved their product and service quality. These brands have learned to improve their quality, with the lowest cost of raw material and manufacturing. They are developing creative and innovative brands to compete with the international brands.

Chapter 7 - Lunch is Never JUST LUNCH

In today's world, societies are moving towards a greater mutual connection. The increasing globalization has created a challenge of how people of different societies, and cultural backgrounds should effectively communicate. People are facing issues like how to communicate while keeping cultural awareness in mind. Therefore, the field of communication has evolved so much, and has gained a huge amount of attention.

Chinese represent one of the largest cultural groups of the world. An understanding of how to effectively communicate with the Chinese is essential for any business deal. Communicating and working with the Chinese is quite a challenge. Therefore, before starting any negotiation with the Chinese, it is vital to know their customs. Respecting these customs are necessary for further communication, and if not followed, your business negotiation may fail.

CHINA

Chinese culture is very different from the rest of the world. Although negotiation around the world may be the same, ways of communication and behavior differ greatly. These differences are followed and respected, and this allows both the parties to build a successful relationship. Some people say that good manners make a good business, and that's exactly how things work in China. Making a good impression is the first thing you need, in order to build good relationships and good opportunities.

Businessmen from the West, when dealing with the Chinese sometimes mistakenly associate the cultural traits with their character and behavior in negotiations. Chinese business etiquettes are closer to the West as compared to Japan's. However, the basic difference between the Western culture and the Chinese is the maintenance of proper hierarchical order and dependence on one individual, to act as a spokesperson for the whole group.

Although Chinese people are found to be very reserved at times, they are generally really easy to approach. It is easy to start a conversation with them. However, getting the relationship to go in the right direction will take time.

Don't push them. Be patient and let them be in control of how things go. All you have to do is be yourself.

The Chinese Negotiation

The concept of negotiation is a foreign input to the Chinese culture. In traditional Chinese, the term ***tan pan*** is used, which translates ***tan*** (discussion) and ***pan*** (making judgment). Negotiating with the Chinese is a diligent task, and you don't want to make it harder by not being prepared. When you get your team together, prepare for the negotiations to improve your chances of success in the Chinese market. Assemble your team before any meeting takes place. Make sure that your team possesses leadership skills and consistency. Cultural elements such as role relationships, time perspectives, and communication styles all come together under the term of negotiation.

In order to run businesses smoothly, it is crucial that you do your homework before conducting business with the Chinese. Study about the company you are scheduled to meet. Chinese people will expect you to be prepared for the meeting. Make sure that you have at least 20 copies of your proposal ready to hand out. Also, make sure that presentation materials should be in black and white. The Chinese people are known to plan meticulously and if they are aware of you coming to visit, then they make sure to study your business inside out.

Between all the negotiating, the Chinese are still figuring whether to do business with you or not. You need to convince them that your company is devoted to the Chinese market, and you look forward to working with them. Show them that you are open and honest, and take time to get to know them. Negotiating with the Chinese is a mixture of hard-nosed bargaining, relationship building, and banqueting. When negotiating with the Chinese, you have to be extremely polite, understanding, open to discussions, and respectful to their cultural differences.

The primary aim in Chinese negotiations is to get concessions that favor them. One of the most important elements of negotiating with the Chinese people is to use the give-and-get approach to reach an agreement. Nobody loses face; both sides gain face. Chinese negotiators begin negotiations by showing humility and deference. This is to present an image of vulnerability and weakness. You are expected to help them through the process, by offering concessions to overcome their weaknesses.

Many westerners, when negotiating in China think that getting the contract signed is the main goal. However, the Chinese think differently. For them, developing a relationship is the primary objective of any negotiation. Foreign businessmen are not aware of this, and they jump right into the business deal. The Chinese require that feeling of being comfortable in dealing with you, before they can think of signing or closing a business deal.

When the Chinese are taking their time in signing the deal, you may start to grow restless. You become impatient and you start losing your chill. Always know that the Chinese often use the clock as a negotiating tool. They believe that foreign businessmen seem to be in a rush to get the deal done. Therefore, the Chinese purposely control the negotiation as per passing time. They do not equate the passing of time with the loss of money or loss of opportunity.

Sometimes, when the Chinese are negotiating a contract, they might sign the agreement sooner than others. However, that is when they begin with the harder negotiation. Many Chinese believe that contracts are flexible even after signing them. A foreign businessman tries to negotiate under a tight time frame. This is intolerable to the Chinese. The larger the project, the Chinese will want to discuss it from every possible angle. The Chinese method of doing things is called a grid or web approach. This involves many considerations. Their attitudes and behavior are often beyond your understandings of a Westerner. When things are not going well, the Chinese will delay the proceedings by using different explanations and tactics, rather than admitting that it is not working out. If the problems are not resolved, then the whole project diminishes and dies.

In China, policy changes are likely to occur without warning. It is necessary for foreign business people to keep an open mind and be very flexible. Above all this, you must be patient and not show anger or frustration. You must practice your best poker face before beginning any negotiation with the Chinese. Once they feel the vibes that you are uncomfortable, they will exploit your weakness.

Their decisions will take a long time, either because of the lack of urgency or because there are a number of negotiations taking place with the competitors. Chinese negotiators question everything. They prefer to establish a strong relationship before closing a deal. They ask about things several times. The Chinese are not known to resolve issues. They do not take decisions at the negotiating table.

Decisions are made after the meeting. It is also a custom for the Chinese to informally drop hints, and make inquiries outside the meeting rooms. Another point to keep in mind about the Chinese is that they do not like surprises. They must be briefed in advance about the subject that is about to be discussed. The agenda made must be followed accordingly. Foreign visitors are to remain polite, cooperative and demonstrate goodwill by following the local customs, as much as possible. When you are the guest of a Chinese, let them lead you around.

The biggest difference between the Chinese and Westerners is the way they think. Westerners think of individuals in straight lines, whereas the Chinese think of groups and circles. These differences have an influence on the present behavior of the Chinese people and their goals. It has an impact on the essence of the Chinese way of negotiating, which makes things go slower and take longer, than the Western behavior. Chinese negotiators typically switch topics without having a connection and without reaching a solid point.

Business Lunch Or Dinner Can Get You A Deal

Conducting business in China is a process of building relationships. In order to build a successful relationship, you will often need to attend several business lunches or dinners, hosted by different business partners. When you are on a business lunch or dinner, there are some ethics the Chinese expect from you. You can build a certain level of trust and comfort at these lunches or dinners.

They expect you to respect their eating manners and practices. Some practices vary from place to place in China; however, some standard elements are the same, for conducting business in China. When you are attending a business meeting in China, it is crucial that you arrive early or at least, arrive on time. The Chinese believe that being late means that you are disrespecting them.

The Chinese do not appreciate anyone being late. The first thing that the Chinese notice is time management. While attending a business meeting, make sure you follow the dress code. You should wear a suit to a formal business meeting if they are wearing it too. But if the Chinese opt for a casual look, you should follow too. There are no hard and fast rules to dress codes, as long as you do not stand out among them.

Chinese dining is mostly conducted at a round table, and this certainly does not mean that it is a casual meeting. There are important people at the table. When people sit at the table for a meeting, the host sits facing towards the door. And if the table is rectangle, the host will sit in the middle of the table. To identify the host, the seat will have a folded napkin shaped in a crane on the plate in front of the seat.

The primary guest of the host is to sit on the host's left. It is a safe choice to wait until you have been invited to sit, rather than you sit on a wrong seat. That would just be disrespecting the host. Once all the members of the meeting have been seated, it is now time to order food. If a menu has not been presented at the table, make sure to expect a lengthy discussion on what to order.

Keep in mind not to order any American food, as this is an offensive gesture. China is known to have the best food in the world, therefore, be open to trying new dishes that your host recommends. After you have placed your order, you begin with the conversation. Most negotiations are barely done at business lunch or dinners. The whole purpose of the business lunch or dinner is to know each other, and build a comfort zone with each other.

Keep your conversation light and pleasant. Compliment the food at the table and discuss your hometown or Chinese landscapes etc. Expect that the Chinese may ask personal questions, such as your age, income, or marital status etc. The Chinese do not consider this rude and in fact, it is a great conversation builder. Finally, the food has arrived. When the food is set on the table, do not begin eating your food immediately.

Follow the lead of the host. The host will begin with a toast to the friendship building with the guest. The glass will be filled with either wine or baijiu. You can drink from the glass, once the toast has been offered. One important etiquette while toasting is to clink your glass lower than the rim of the host's glass. This is a sign of respect towards the host of the lunch. You're done with the toast and it is now time to begin the meal.

Chinese meals are served family-style. This is your cue to begin eating. In China, except soup, every course is eaten with chopsticks. It is considered bad etiquette to tap your chopsticks on the side of your plate. It is disrespectful to point with your chopstick, suck on a chopstick, poke at dishes with your chopstick or drop your chopsticks. In China, it is completely acceptable to slurp, burp and belch while eating. This is a sign that you are enjoying the food. Also, it is a common practice to use toothpicks while eating. You can do so but with your hand covering your mouth. China has a principle to eat a little of everything. You are supposed to taste every dish served, whether you are familiar with it or not. It may be dog meat, blood, scorpions, snake, or even grasshoppers. The host will feel offended, if you have not touched any dish.

One of the eating manners in China, is that it is necessary for you to leave food on your plate. A clean plate is a signal that you have been left unsatisfied. At the ending of the meal, fruit or dessert will be served. This is to signal that the meal is about to end. Meals officially end when the host stands up, and thanks the attendees. Hot towels are presented at the end of the meal, and that is when you know that the business lunch or dinner has come to an end.

Lastly, it is rude to tip.

The host of the dinner pays for everything at the business lunch in China. The above-mentioned rules are little gestures that will help you build the trust of your Chinese partner. Except for lunch and dinner, there are more processes to follow, before a Chinese can trust in you as much as to close a deal with you.

Gaining Chinese Trust

Trust has a different definition in China. 'Trust' in China translates as 'thinking with the heart'. It tells us about the deep importance of this emotional state. For the Chinese, analytical processes and strategic thinking are the top priority. The importance of thinking and focusing, is a cherished aspect of Chinese life. It constitutes wisdom, proficiency, and maturity in life.

Trust and degrees of trust represent the Chinese in such a way that it is coded in the Chinese system. Gaining trust in Chinese is about willingness and discipline in the way we handle our emotions, combined with a consciousness of our connection to others. Trust is basically the ability to apply logic and emotions to the related task.

Above all, trust means observing the methods to avoid

loss of reputation and acceptance of the social groups. In China, social acceptance is vital in life. For example, if two people are together and one person facilitates the loss of the other, that person is harming himself. That person is rejecting his own hopes and destroying his own reputation, and compromising his present and future.

In conclusion, you need to be mindful. You have to ensure that the commitment relating to trust is deep. It must not be based on availability, adversity, or distance. One must be wholeheartedly willing to participate in the business reputation. One needs to earn others' trust in China, in order to do business with them. Without trust, the Chinese may read some other hidden purpose of what you do. This is harmful to the development of the business.

The Chinese government has made significant efforts to encourage entrepreneurship and small business ownership. Building your trust in the Chinese market is a challenge, and you will need time to build trust with them. *"Guanxi"* is the term used to describe the relationship-development process in China that has been already explained in the earlier chapters. In the West, professional relationships are built after the first introduction.

But this is not the case in China. Many Westerners become a little frustrated because of the long wait. However, they do not realize that the Chinese need time to develop a positive relationship. It usually takes weeks and several meetings, before a Chinese businessman builds a trustful relationship. You must be patient and respect the Chinese practice to feel more confident doing business with people, and trust to deliver quality work and carry out honest communication. *Guanxi's* importance in China has developed as a result of the many implications of the rule of law. In the past, China had lacked a rule of law because did not provide China with the legal protections like the West. China then developed another means to ensure trust in personal and business matters. When the Chinese develop *Guanxi* with a person, they do not take advantage of him.

And if they do so, they lose the respect of others in the group, and eventually lose their trust. It seems obvious that the *Guanxi* technology is distinct in the Chinese characteristics. This may be why many scholars have related it to the Chinese culture. There is a widespread use of personal relationships among the Chinese, and the uniqueness in the way of using personal relationships.

In fact, this might be the reason as to why the word *Guanxi* is used to describe the Chinese culture, instead of describing a general system of networks. For these reasons, a Chinese company feels more comfortable doing business with a company they have a strong connection with. They believe that it is far easier for them to trust their business partner. This goes vice versa.

Foreign companies need to develop a strong *Guanxi* with the Chinese. This will help your company to flourish. You won't face problems in doing business in China.

Develop And Maintain Guanxi

Developing *Guanxi* is important in doing business in China. However, it is not that easy to develop and you need to be calm. Being completely present in China is necessary when developing and maintaining it. It will be helpful to have a native Chinese responsible to develop these relationships. A native Chinese will be familiar and comfortable with the Chinese norms of developing Guanxi.

This Chinese representative will be seen in formal and informal meetings and will be put forward to customers and government agencies, to build strong positive relationships. The maintenance of *Guanxi* requires continuous social interaction. Social visits, dinner invitations, gift-giving help in maintaining it. Frequent interaction is essential in a Guanxi.

Without these gestures, it may fade. Different Guanxi relations build opportunities for interaction. These increase the feeling of unity between the parties and thus makes it easier for it to develop. Multiple Guanxi are more fused, than a single one. The closer the Guanxi, the higher is the expectation of its reliability by both parties.

Maintaining a *Guanxi* also depends on reliability and trustworthiness. Unreliability can transform a close Guanxi into a distant one in no time. Once a Guanxi has been established, you need to invest time and effort to develop the relation. To maintain a Guanxi connection, it is important to reinforce the personal relationship with your partner. Guanxi once lost is not easy to gain back.

Sincerity and frankness are essential. In order to do this,

you must acquire an in-depth knowledge of your partner's personal needs and demands. Continuous reinforcement of personal attachment for Guanxi relations is also necessary. *Guanxi* is not limited to the business sector. In China, you need to develop Guanxi even with your tax authority and other organizations. This mutual trust helps to facilitate any dealings you have with the outside stakeholders.

This does not mean that you participate in corrupt practices, but this just means that conducting a smooth business and a healthy business relationship becomes easier. In the maintenance of a Guanxi, it is important to know not to overuse it, as the other party may feel a burden. One must also remember his obligations to the Guanxi and respond when called upon.

As competition rises day by day, it is hard to keep up with the growing business sector around the world. *Guanxi* is one factor that can help make the competition run smoothly without any issues. Changes in modern Chinese businesses will continue to shape the economy in China. It will bring changes and people will find new ways to cope up.

The use and definition of Guanxi will also evolve with these changes. However, one thing is certain though, that whatever the year or decade, or however, the business sector turns out to be, Guanxi will remain an important and inevitable part of conducting business in China.

Chapter 8 - The Mouse Chases The Cat

China is a large country, both population-wise and area-wise. The customs and traditions of its people vary by geography and ethnicity. Ancient Chinese culture is more than 5,000 years old. Chinese cultural history offers diversity and variety. The population of the country is around 1.4 billion, and they represent 56 different ethnic groups.

Some important ethnicities include Hans, Tibetans, Mongols, Manchus, Naxi, and the Hezhen. Chinese culture includes diversity in religion, food, style, language, marriage, music morals, and many other things that make up how people act and interact with each other. The Chinese language, literature, philosophy, and politics are still counted as the most influential elements.

Chinese culture has managed to retain its uniqueness, until the growth of Western culture in the mid-19th Century. Building personal relationships is one of the main elements of doing business in China. You need to invest time in getting to know your contact. However, when your senior executives are rushing to close the deal in China, it is a bad approach. It would be better if you send your junior members to prepare the ground, before the senior executives reach out to talk business. The Chinese culture is held by four thick threads. For more than 5,000 years, the Chinese business negotiations have demonstrated their culture. The first thread is *Agrarianism*. Two-thirds of the Chinese people live in rural areas, and they work as labor for rice and wheat cultivation.

Chinese have a tradition of peasant farming. Chinese society stresses the importance of agriculture and farming. It was once the most common form of socio-economic organization for most of human history. It is based on groups and not on individuals. Their survival is based entirely on group cooperation. This depicts that the Chinese are loyal to their family and bind their groups together.

Chinese people who have been born in the countryside have maintained their agrarian values throughout generations. The second thread of the Chinese culture is *Morality*. The teachings of Confucius were the foundation of Chinese education for 2,000 years, and during those two millenniums, Confucianism maintained a society that is organized and lives under a moral code.

This society would be prosperous, and politically stable and safe from any attacks. To understand the importance of hierarchy in Chinese society, let's take the story of Cheng Han-cheng and his wife. According to a Chinese scholar Dau-lin Hsu, Cheng's wife had the guts to beat up her mother-in-law. This was categorized as a heinous crime, due to which Cheng and his wife were both skinned alive. Their flesh was displayed at the gates of various cities, and their bones were burned to ashes.

These moral values are expressed in the Chinese negotiating style. Chinese negotiators are more focused on the means of the negotiation, rather than the end. They are concerned about the process rather than the goal. While the West believe the truth as they see it, argue over it, and get angry about it; the Chinese, however, believe that the way is hard to find, and they rely on haggling to settle the differences.

The third thread is ***Chinese pictographic language***. Just as Western children learn to read and write Roman letters and numbers, Chinese children learn to memorize pictorial characters. In Chinese, words are depicted as pictures rather than a sequence of letters. Therefore, learning these pictorial characters tend to build a holistic processing of information in children. Michael Harris Bond, a professor at the Chinese University pointed that the Chinese children have the ability to see the bigger picture, however, the American children have the ability to focus on the tiny details. The fourth and last thread is Chinese people's *wariness of foreigners*. This has been learned through the hard way from the long and violent history of attacks.

China has often fallen victim to internal fights, civil wars, and the flow of empires. This combination produces distrust towards the rule of law and the rules of the country overall. It is believed that the Chinese only trust their families and their bank accounts. These four threads are the reason as to why the Chinese are the way they are. To deal and negotiate with the Chinese, it is important to learn about them and their culture.

Negotiation in China

China's booming economy and growing international consumer influence have made the role of negotiation in international business more important than ever. An appropriate skill set for negotiating in China is in high demand in the internal market.

Although negotiating is a universal practice, communication and behavior depend on the country. Therefore, for a successful negotiation, knowing the culture and its differences are required. The Chinese word for negotiation, *tan pan*, means *"to discuss"* and *"to judge"*. In China, negotiation is a process for building trust between the two parties, so they can work together and benefit each other. The negotiation process enables the parties to reach an understanding, regarding a specific issue or transaction in a way that each side benefits mutually. Doing negotiation in China is more like running without knowing where the finish line actually is.

People participating in this marathon need endurance and perseverance, to make sure the process is through. Americans think of negotiation, as a process where complex situations are discussed and broken down to smaller parts to easily tackle them. Once an agreement is reached, papers are signed to close the deal. However, in China, the negotiations go around in circles and drag on; from discussing the price to quantity and never settling on anything. Before entering into a Chinese negotiation, it is necessary that you leave your expectations aside, as this will lead to frustration and error in judgment.

When adapting Chinese-style negotiations, foreign partners need to settle specific issues and contract terms with the building of interpersonal relationships. To compete with a Chinese negotiation framework means to understand and accommodate the Chinese style of approach, in order to make a strategic plan that works on every level. When negotiating anywhere, or in China, for the most part, know where you stand before proceeding with anything.

Knowing your position can make negotiation easier. Find a strong negotiation team that is aligned, and aware of the limitations and restrictions behind the deal. Make sure that your teammates are aware of the sensitive issues, the non-negotiable conditions, and the giveaway items that may come up during the meeting. There are many ways to find an agreement that all can agree upon.

Preparing the team beforehand will ensure that everyone has their stance on different topics. It's all about the relationships in China, therefore, overly aggressive and very direct tactics are damaging when it comes to negotiating with the Chinese. Having a strong team that knows how to engage with them is highly advantageous. If you are personally involved in any negotiations, it is important to understand the proper etiquette to do so.

Concepts like saving face are really critical, and deals can be made or broken by the lack of sensitivity in these areas. It is crucial that you do not insult anyone or their ideas. You must also respect others' status in the business and not treat them as juniors. If you are facing your first negotiation with the Chinese, you have no idea of how difficult it is to deal with them. The younger generation in China can easily speak English, however, the older population is seldom educated abroad and therefore do not easily understand English.

To make your negotiations easy and smooth in China, the best pick is to have a translator in hand. Your translator must have a vast knowledge of the subject you are planning to discuss. For example, if you are talking finance, make sure that you have someone who is aware of the terminologies, and who can talk profits, depreciation, and other financial terms.

China is known about its formalities in the country. However, what is unusual is that the meetings are missing structure. In the West, meetings come with an agenda and expected outcomes, whereas, in China, meetings begin with a long conversation that covers a broad range of topics. Thus when talking about business in China, it is important that you come prepared to talk about a number of different topics. For example, if you are planning to talk about the production of your product, make sure that the topics will include shipping logistics, payment arrangements, and factory inspections, etc. Negotiations in China are never over. You can have the owner of the company fly in to sign the papers to close the deal and believe that it is all done, but then the next day you find out that they have issues in the agreement, and need to discuss changes in the contract. Chinese companies are loaded with cash; however, they don't have the knowledge and the experience.

Therefore many Chinese companies hire Western businesses to incorporate their knowledge and connections. The Chinese are masters of learning and they often ask very good questions through which you can learn from them, and they can learn from you. Therefore, regardless of what business you present, be prepared to showcase your experience, your breadth of knowledge, and your credentials to support it. Your Chinese partner may not let you know, but they consider it during their evaluation.

Doing business in China means that you are putting your company in a culture that is not masked in secrecy. They have a very open business policy. The Chinese are known to build relationships, over a period of time. For the Chinese, they are not worth the paper without a good relationship with the parties.

After understanding the negotiation style of the Chinese, you will be able to appreciate the differences of the Chinese companies, their culture, traditions, and work ethics behind their communication styles. Below are some points that should always be remembered to increase your chances to successfully negotiate with the Chinese partners.

- Show concern for their personal lives. Keep it above the business deal.
- Try and get to know all the cultures of over 50 ethnic groups. Learn about your partner's individuality.
- Give gifts. They are a form of building trust and understanding the Chinese business etiquette.
- Try different Chinese cuisines, even if you do not prefer them.

- Respect the positions of your partners. Make sure that you send a representative who is equal to their rank.
- Be on time for a meeting. The Chinese value punctuality, and arriving on time shows your respect towards their culture.
- Build a personal relationship. If they can't trust you on a personal level, they won't trust you on a business level.
- Have patience. Do not rush into signing the agreement.
- Establish a long-term relationship. The Chinese do business with those who they trust.

Respect The Chinese View

As previously discussed, the Chinese culture has the highest value overall when doing business deals. Decades of communist rule can affect the most personal human interaction. But this is exactly the influence of collectivism on the lives of the Chinese up to this date, which is different from communism. Being a western business leader, your basic need is to respect this influence and culture, and understand that your Chinese partners may not define the value of culture in the same way that you do in the west. Although some of the Western individualism has entered into the Chinese culture; for many, individual accomplishments will still be secondary to organizational and family obligations. One of the biggest challenges of doing business with Chinese partners is to understand who the real decision-maker is. The biggest difference between the Western and the Chinese business culture is in the decision making.

It is not always clear who dictates the final outcome. The person you are negotiating with may not be the person in charge, and may be reporting back to the real decision-makers who is the force behind the scenes. The Chinese are not known to make quick decisions. Rapid decision making is the sign of an aggressive manager in the West. However, haste in China is the sign of an idiot. The Chinese are known to get in control.

They like the idea that they are in control of the business deal. In China, people do not like to say *"No"*, or even admit that they do not understand anything. They are known to pretend that they are not dumb and are the smartest amongst everyone else. They want to have this perception that the deal depends on them, and without them, the business would be at a loss. Just like *"Tom and Jerry"*, the famous cartoon. Tom and Jerry are two of the most honored cartoon characters of all time. It was created by William Hanna and Joseph Barbera. The first protagonist, Tom, is a blue-grey haired cat while the second protagonist, Jerry, is a small, brown house mouse. The story revolves around the never-ending battle of a chase between a housecat and a brown mouse.

The episodes though show different variations of the original theme; the cat chasing the mouse. In the cartoon, it is shown that Tom the cat, is chasing after the mouse. Tom is shown playing the dominant role who is overpowering Jerry, due to which Jerry is unable to live a life of peace in a house. Tom is unable to catch Jerry though, because Jerry is smarter and more cunning than Tom.

But if you take a look at it closely, the actual concept behind it is the total opposite. Jerry, the mouse is the actual reason why Tom can't live in peace. Tom thinks that he is in control of the house, but actually, it's Jerry who is controlling Tom. Tom has the feeling of dominance that he is overpowering Jerry, but in reality, it is Jerry who is overpowering Tom with his little mischief.

The same idea is put forward with the Chinese. The Chinese have a nature that they like being in control. Therefore, when you are going to negotiate with the Chinese, the best tactic to deal with such a situation is to let the Chinese feel that they are in control. But under the table, it should be you pulling the strings. Let the Chinese make the decisions, but make sure that the decisions made favor your needs.

This will give the impression that the Chinese are in control, however, you are taking the lead in reality. You can start by placing an artificial deadline. It is an obvious manipulation, however, it will work well at most times. At the very beginning of the negotiation process, the Chinese set a fixed date for executing the contract. The data set is far in advance and this helps to ensure that the parties are in good faith, and can reach the agreement mentioned on the contract.

You can set your deadline to an earlier date and give the impression that the pressure of the pending signing ceremony will result in a crucial concession, which will favor your side instead of theirs. Another situation may be that if the Chinese use the *"wear 'em down technique"*. This is where the Chinese go back over and over again in many different ways to wear the opponent down. These demands are mostly ridiculous and illogical. You should refuse to participate. They are there to take your eyes off the ball and you lose your patience, by the time it comes down to the real negotiation. You can firmly state your position and not give in to the Chinese, until they agree or move closer to your position.

Also, make it clear that there will be no changes made to the contract after the signing has taken place, and any attempt made by the Chinese in this regard will be further treated as a material breach. The Chinese are well known for using the signing of the contract, as the start of a new negotiating process and not the termination of the contract. Negotiating a good agreement with the Chinese, however, is a difficult and time-consuming process.

The fact that the Chinese business culture is filled with suspicion should be a lesson for every company that is planning to do business in the country. Those companies that are looking forward to entering the Chinese market must keep in mind that the laws including corporate partnerships and joint ventures are weak, and are always at a disadvantage to a foreign country. Therefore, picking the right Chinese business partner, and negotiating the best possible terms are the essential keys to success.

Chapter 9 - The Deal is Never Done

By now, we have developed the fact that China is the fastest growing economy in the world. To maintain relationships with the customers in China, we need to be aware of the culture and rituals that take place among the Chinese. To be able to build a good relationship with the Chinese, you need to understand what makes or breaks a Chinese deal.

Business people need to be sensitive towards Chinese culture and learn how it can impact their businesses. When doing business in China, you are likely going to face problems. If you are looking forward to doing business in China, you need to understand just how the locals conduct themselves in business relationships. These relationships differ on many stages but when dealing with Chinese, business relationships change for good, and become even more complex and personal.

It is often noted by the foreign businesspeople that the real negotiating begins after a contract has been signed. Most problems occur from the fact that government officials and company executives have limited authority, and they interpret the provisions of contracts according to their cultural, political, and economic point of view. When establishing a relationship with the Chinese, it is very important to come across with faith.

After you have established the initial relationship, it is important that you remain very careful in taking the next step, because the deal is not closed. It is an affair which can make you or break you. Doing business with the Chinese is an ongoing process. The Chinese dislike the get in and get out attitude. They might make a deal with you, but this will not help build a good reputation. Many Western business representatives have walked out of a meeting with the Chinese, believing that the deal was closed.

However, that is not the case. The Chinese tend to agree with you, nod their heads, and say yes to the conditions you put forward. But that does not mean that the deal is closed. To the Chinese, *"face"* is important. For the Chinese, making a verbal commitment is the key to establishing a relationship.

Keeping Face

As mentioned in the previous chapters, *"Guanxi"* is the personal connection between two people. It is the foundation of all business deals in China. It is necessary to build trust with someone, in order to do business with them. But alongside building new relationships, it is necessary to maintain the old ones as well. Just like an old friend, it is common that you offer gifts to your business contacts, go for dinners, and attend social events.

These gestures will strengthen the Guanxi relationship you have, and open doors to opportunities that would have been closed to you. When in a Chinese business relationship, it is important that you see it as a partnership of equality, and treat the other party as an equal. Acting superior or putting someone down is aggressive according to the Chinese perspective.

It is known that being too aggressive will lead to a *"loss of face"* and can cause an end to a relationship. *"Face"* or *"Mianzi"* is an important factor in the Chinese culture. It is all about how the people around you perceive you. Because of the importance of Guanxi, you need to always have a good face. Chinese culture is densely hierarchical which is why you need to show the people around you an ample amount of respect. In the Western culture, *"face"* is basically reputation. In China, face is a complicated system of shame and stature measurement. Saving face is the priority for the Chinese, and losing face is a cause of great pain and concern. For the Chinese, causing someone to lose face on purpose can build you an enemy for life.

As a foreigner, it is assumed and accepted that you do not mean to cause someone to lose face. As a potential client, you will probably receive a lot of Mianzi, when looking for a partner for your potential business. They constantly show you face to prove that they are worthy of your business. They can do this through compliments or even through gifts.

Some common ways to give face include:

- Giving high compliments often and freely.
- Praising someone in front of elders and superiors.
- Giving high marks on evaluation forms.
- Giving an expensive gift.
- Inviting someone for an expensive meal.

Some of the face-losing situations that you should avoid include:

- Calling someone out on a lie.
- Revealing someone's lack of knowledge.
- Not showing proper respect to elders or superiors.
- Turning down an invitation.
- Criticizing openly, challenging someone, or disagreeing with someone.
- Being publicly angry.

According to an Asian scholar, Ting-Toomey, *"face"* is a strategy that protects self-respect and individual identity. Face-saving activities are the rights that protect the individual's role in the Guanxi network. The Chinese prefer to do business with people that they trust the most.

To nurture newly built relationships, the Chinese have mastered the art of hospitality, flattery, real friendship, and sometimes false friendship. While relationships need trust, flexibility, and loyalty, they also create obligations.

The perspective about relationships within the Chinese is a double-edged sword, because they are known to make new demands, reopen contracts, renegotiate settled terms in the contract, and demand for new concessions. Just when you tend to believe that the negotiation is finished as you sign the contract, it turns out it is not true in Chinese negotiations. Your Chinese partner sees the agreement, as the beginning of the relationship.

Learning Mandarin

As mentioned a couple of times throughout the book, Chinese business etiquette and culture are different from the western world. When learning about these practices, it is a plus to learn and speak Mandarin. With China being the largest country in the world, with regards to the global population, Chinese is the world's most spoken language.

Around 1.2 billion people identify Chinese as their first language. However, Chinese itself is a group of various intelligible languages, but the most common one is Mandarin. As China is surpassing Western economy, Mandarin is also enjoying an increase in commercial circles.

To develop a strong relationship with your Chinese partner, it is important that you learn Mandarin. Developing a strong relationship with the Chinese partners usually leads to a meeting at the negotiating table. Learning to speak with the Chinese in their native tongue, shows your respect towards them. This will not only help you avoid embarrassment but also help you relax and focus on building your success. Chinese people discuss matters besides businesses, such as your likes and hobbies. This is how the Chinese judge your character's worthiness to conduct business with you.

People would assume that learning Mandarin is enough and business mandarin is almost similar. They might think that business mandarin is not as useful, and they tend to ignore the language. It is true that Mandarin and Business Mandarin are the same language. However, it is not entirely the same when it comes down to mandarin terms and Chinese business etiquettes.

Understanding Chinese Holidays and Festivals

Chinese religion has many different expressions. It does not have a formal infrastructure. However, Chinese religion is a term that describes various interactions of religious and philosophical traditions that are influential in China. This includes Chinese folk religion, Confucianism, Taoism, and

Buddhism.

Several traditional Chinese holidays and festivals are celebrated throughout the year. Learning and understanding these Chinese holidays build a sense of respect towards your partner. They sense the feeling that you respect their holidays, and are aware of what matters to them. Sending gifts on special occasions enhance your Guanxi towards your partner. Therefore, knowing the Chinese holidays is crucial when building a relationship in China.

The most well-known Chinese holiday is the Chinese New Year. It is celebrated in Chinatowns all over the world. Chinese and non-Chinese people, both look forward to this traditional holiday to enjoy the cultural aspects of China. Other holidays celebrate the seasons and honor the deceased ancestors.

Chinese New Year

This is one of the most well-known celebrations all over the world. It is also known as the Lunar New Year or the Spring Festival. The Chinese New Year is celebrated during the first three days of the first lunar month, and it is celebrated worldwide. However, the celebrations may go on for sixteen days. The preparations start seven days before New Year's Eve.

Traditionally, the houses are cleaned and decorated with red lanterns, red carpets, and New Year paintings days before the Chinese New Year. It is celebrated with firecrackers, lanterns, torches, and bonfires to chase away the evil spirits according to Chinese beliefs. Dragon dances and lion dances take place in the streets and other public places throughout the first few days of the Chinese New Year. It is followed with a New Year Eve's Feast, which is a must-do dinner with all the family members.

The Chinese New Year's Day is a good opportunity to send greetings to your partners and clients. You don't need to go all the way for anything elaborate, a phone call or a drop-in would be perfect. If your partner uses email, then send them an e-card with a personalized greeting message. It is a nice time to send a generic greeting to your partners, clients, and customers during the Chinese New Year holiday.

Qingming Festival

Qingming Festival is also known as the Tomb-Sweeping

Day or Pure Brightness Festival. It is the second of 24 solar terms on the traditional Chinese solar calendar. It is a time for people to go out and enjoy the views of spring.

The Qingming Festival is a traditional Chinese festival and an important day of sacrifice for most of the people, to go and sweep tombs of their ancestors and commemorate them. On this auspicious day, the most important act is tomb sweeping to show respect to the ancestors.

During the Qingming Festival, the popular activities that take place are tomb upkeep and repair, spring outings, kite flying, and putting willow branches on gates. People participate in a sport to prevent the cold, and anticipate the arrival of spring.

Since the taboo subject of death is involved, the whole process of Qingming is a private and solemn one. As a non-Chinese, it is best that you do not send any special greetings or gifts, and leave the three-day holiday alone.

National Day

When China was under the imperial rule, National Day was a celebration with regards to the Emperor's birthday or the date of his rise to the throne. Now, National Day in

CHINA

China is held to celebrate the formation of the People's Republic of China.

The first seven days of October are known as the Golden Week. This is a time of travel and leisure, and great celebrations in various parts of China. People from different cities travel to the rural areas to relax, and get away from the busy city routines. Reciprocally, people from the rural areas also travel to the cities, to take part in large celebrations in a city.

Celebrations include military performances, food vendors, live music, and other activities. In different cities, musical and dance concerts are held to celebrate the National Day. On the evening of the National Day, grand fireworks are demonstrated. These fireworks are presented by the Government, and the highest quality rockets are used to fill the sky with sparkling colors.

Your local partners will expect the very least on this holiday; a season's greeting from you. It is a great opportunity to surprise them with a gift. Timing is the key when dealing with the Chinese. Therefore, plan ahead with the support of your local partner, and send in a carefully designed greeting card or gift pack.

To make good use of the Chinese holidays in your business development and corporate communications campaign, you can focus on these pointers:

- Be aware of all the holidays that are coming up, making sure that you see the actual dates of each year.
- Have the best timing for your promotional activities and event planning.
- Differ from everyone else. Create your greeting cards, gifts, and events in a manner to stand out from the rest.

After Closing The Deal

When the Chinese make a commitment, they need to take action. When they take action after making a commitment with you, is when you know that they are moving forward. For example, sending a delegate to your country to experience and further understand your business, or even ship some product for you to examine, etc. When the Chinese take action, you know that they are willing to close the deal.

After you have done the negotiations and the discussions, and have finally closed the deal; according to the Chinese customs, you cannot just leave your partner until the next meeting. You need to stay in contact for any further information that has to be conveyed, or any further action that has to be taken. To present yourself as a customer-centric organization, you need to understand how important great customer service and support is.

Nowadays, customers demand constant accessibility. They want to be served without any delay. The quality of customer support is one of the basic elements of a business. And it is how the potential customer looks at you. Your partners are like your customers, and they do not appreciate waiting. You should ensure that you do not put your Chinese partner on hold, for any reason whatsoever.

You need to be available to them 24/7, as this indicates high responsiveness and commitment. This also indicates that you respect them and take time out to entertain them. The key to success in China is to always stay patient and calm. Showing impatience or anxiety, and modesty in speech, dress, and mannerisms play an important role, when dealing with the Chinese.

Chapter 10 – Fin

The previous chapters have mentioned building the right relationships with the Chinese extensively. But what most businesses do not focus on, is using these relationships to build more relationships for the benefit of their business. People are not aware of why they need Chinese partners. Good Chinese partners contribute to establishing your business in China. The sense of *'connectedness'* in the Chinese context means to live not as an individual but as a *'connected part of networks'*.

Most Chinese people form and maintain a circle of influence, which includes both family and business relationships. It is, therefore, important to understand just how the Chinese form their circles of influence in life, and view friendships and business relations differently. The Chinese have a 'stranger zone' in which they place people outside their 'circles', who are regarded as strangers. The Chinese are known to prefer spending their time and energy within the group of people who fall into their 'circle of influence.'

If you are a person who wishes to form a long-term relationship with the Chinese, it is necessary that you enter their circles, and follow the rules to stay in it. Chinese circles of family and business relationships have separate structures and have many layers. These layers are further known as 'rings' within a circle.

People who are in the outer rings are less important, as compared to the people in the inner rings. However, the yin and yang law means that these positions are not permanent. Relationships can change with time, depending on the circumstances.

The Chinese Business Circle

When dealing with a Chinese business partner, it is important to understand that the Chinese believe business partners should be good friends too. The Chinese business circle consists of friends, colleagues, business associates, and other connections.

The most important relations include friends, business contacts, and government connections. The Chinese invest a lot of time and energy, to nurture and maintain their circles of influence. In reality, most of the eating, gift-giving, and spa treatments are a part of, working to keep these relationships alive. This business circle changes with time and therefore, people from the outer ring shift to the core and vice versa. Successful Chinese are those who possess the art of balancing these relationships within their circle, and position themselves well in the circles of others. Different groups of the Chinese business community have their type of circles, which they build around themselves.

People who are linked with a governmental job have stronger links in the government, the communist party, and related agencies. They form their networks within their business area and do not like spending time mixing around with other business sectors, unless it is necessary to do so. Their business and family circles are independent of each other, despite being interwoven. The Chinese are known to keep personal and professional lives aside.

However, in the private sector, the Chinese have a different kind of circle. The Chinese entrepreneur has a mixed range of people they deal with. Therefore, most of them merge their business and family circles, and their business relationships overlap their other ones, as they run a family business. Chinese entrepreneurs are known to involve family members and relatives in their businesses, because they are believed to be the most trustworthy. The Chinese do not like dealing with strangers. Therefore, they are more comfortable with family working alongside. The real family members and relatives, hold key positions in such a business. One rule to keep in mind is to never do business with a Chinese that has no experience in doing international business.

The risk is too high, and there is a probability that they will not understand your objectives, and therefore, the business relationship will eventually fail. You will need to ask for recommendations and suggestions from the people involved in the industry. Therefore, it is crucial that your potential partner is aware of the approach of doing so. Entering a Chinese business or social 'circle' means to socialize or network with the Chinese.

Western businesspeople make the mistake of gathering and socializing with the people they know. They go to the same functions and invite the same people for parties, and then they complain of feeling alienated. If you ever get the opportunity to attend a Chinese gathering, you should accept the invitation. You may feel as if the occasion is too Chinese, the invitation itself is a gesture that the Chinese are trying to include you in their circle.

If you do not show up, you are giving them the '*Mianzi*'. But if you do show up, you get to observe and bond with more potential partners and make new friends. It requires time and patience to develop a focused relationship with the Chinese.

Once this relationship is developed, it will reward you in the long term. If you spread yourself too much, it will have an opposite effect on the efforts you are making. You need to remember that relationships take time, and if you ignore or fail to maintain a relationship, it can easily be lost.

Depending On Your Chinese Partner

When you have successfully built a relationship with the Chinese, you can consider getting assistance from your Chinese partner. Your Chinese partner can help you ease your business issues by channeling his circle of influence.

Having a close business contact with the Chinese is essential when doing business in China. It can help in navigating local laws and regulations, connecting to government officials, and having in-country marketing expertise. Chinese business contacts can come in handy in many other aspects.

Building Government Relations

It is a good idea to take your Chinese business partner along, when you visit your targeted government official. This gives your company more respect in the eyes of the government officials. You are portraying to the government officials that your Chinese partner is important to your business. This approach to government relations is best for firms that are planning to get involved in joint ventures with the Chinese.

You can use the strengths of your Chinese partner's relationships, and get the benefit of their political connections. This is especially useful when you are trying to get approvals from the government officials. Get your company's senior executives to be directly involved in government relations, so they can clearly understand how things work in China.

Sometimes, when senior executives presume that things cannot be done, it is mostly because the China team does not know how to do it. Some executives may also challenge you, on the amount of effort that you put in your government relationships. Developing government contacts takes a lot of time and effort. Only then your business will be able to develop relationships with Chinese government officials.

Recruiting Local Staff

Hiring a local employee is a tough task. It comprises of following a specific procedure. This includes making the right employment contract, knowing the nature of employment, understanding the individual income tax and other benefits, and learning about the public holidays in China. Other aspects include learning paid annual leaves of the employees, employment termination procedures, and expected HR policies.

Your Chinese business partner can help you get through the entire recruitment process, without you having to experience the hassle. Your local partner knows how to find the right fit for your company. Using your partner for the recruitment process will help you get the right employees in your company.

Developing Distributors and Buying Agents

When finding a distributor or an agent in China, you

would want to search in the most easily accessible cities. Working with local wholesale parties, agents, or distributors is a basic need when exporting to China.

Your Chinese partner helps you with entering the new markets of China. They know the language and have experienced business contacts on the governmental level to help you in your business venture. They are aware of the Chinese mindset and can deal with them on a more accurate perspective. Furthermore, to build a strong international business relationship with your Chinese partner, you need to focus on some business ethics.

Relationships are everything in China, and when conducting business in China, we need to build the right relationships. As mentioned previously in the book, *Guanxi* is the basic requirement in a relationship. It means to have personal trust and a strong relationship with someone, whether a business partner or a family member. This includes moral obligations and exchanging favors.

We already know that the Chinese are slow in building relationships. However, when the trust is built, the Chinese want to move on a quicker pace. To build a longlasting and strong relationship, it is necessary to understand these factors to gain success. However, with the increase of the economic reforms and changes in China, only Guanxi is not enough.

When building relationships with partners, you need to make sure that they are open to new and fresh ideas. Whether they are agents, distributors, or other partners, you need to make sure that they have enough experience in the local market, and are familiar with the differences in the local consumer market to carry out the new ideas. On top of it all, your business partner must possess the resources and relationships that can complement yours.

However, relationships come with their fair share of risks. Trust and communication are essential when building a strong relationship. To sum up the entire process, here are some useful practices that can be followed to maintain a relationship with your Chinese partner.

- Understand the objectives. Avoid rushing into a relationship without considering the objectives. It is necessary to understand what the Chinese party wants to accomplish.

- You need to implement those business practices that have made many other US companies successful in dealing with China.
- Choose the right business partner. Selecting the wrong business partner is one of the major mistakes, when dealing with Chinese companies. The right partner will help flourish your business in many ways, whereas, the wrong business partner will not be able to handle the pressures of your business.
- Make sure always to have a strong legal foundation for business relationships. The Chinese use the phrase, *"we know the law, but that is not how things are done in China."* This is a 'no lose' situation for the Chinese partner. It is common for a Chinese partner to use the 'failure to comply with the law' game to get concessions from the U.S Company. Having strong legal support can keep you on the safe side when building relationships.
- Understand the role of contracts. In China, contracts are used as a tool in building relationships. Therefore, they are being renegotiated even after they are signed. The Westerners should be prepared

to respond to long negotiations in alignment with the interest of both the parties.

- Like mentioned above, build a government relations strategy. The Chinese government is involved in every aspect of Chinese businesses. As a result, the US companies need to develop relationships with key government officials. Your Chinese partner is responsible for introducing you to such officials, intermediaries, lawyers, etc.
- Develop *Guanxi*. It has been focused on numerously in this book how important Guanxi is. China is not a place where individuals function alone. They function in a group and with relationships. Therefore, to maintain the right relationship, developing and implementing Guanxi is essential.
- Build a personal relationship with the Chinese partner on a day-to-day basis. The better the relationship, the better the venture will turn out to be. This process is known as '*jiao pengyou*'.
- You need to participate in the duties and obligations of both the parties actively. When managing a relationship with a Chinese partner, it is necessary to have a local presence. This will give you a

greater chance of success in the Chinese market. This active participation is essential for building relationships and also builds accountability.

- Appreciate the Chinese negotiating style. We have acknowledged it earlier that the Chinese have a different negotiating style, as compared to the West. As a result, the Westerners need to understand how the Chinese negotiate, and should follow along with their business ethics. This will not only allow the company to avoid frustration, but will also enhance your relationship with them. These lengthy negotiations are a means of testing the western party to determine, if they are worth the investment or are just another fool entering the Chinese market.

CHINA

Bibliography

Farrall - 2008 - Global Privacy in Flux Illuminating Privacy acros.pdf. (n.d.). Retrieved from https://ijoc.org/index.php/ijoc/article/viewFile/370/228

Farrall, K. N. (2008). Global Privacy in Flux: Illuminating Privacy across Cultures in China and the U.S., 38.

Farrell, B., VandeVusse, A., & Ocobock, A. (2012). Family change and the state of family sociology. *Current Sociology*, *60*(3), 283–301. Retrieved from https://doi.org/10.1177/0011392111425599

Kanellos, M. (n.d.). China: Bursting with brainpower. Retrieved January 30, 2019, from https://www.zdnet.com/article/china-bursting-with-brainpower/

Lee, R. Y.-P., & Bond, M. H. (1998). Personality and Roommate Friendship in Chinese Culture. *Asian Journal of Social Psychology*, *1*(2), 179–190. Retrieved from https://doi.org/10.1111/1467-839X.00012

Poon, L. (n.d.). How Chinese Homebuyers Are Changing America's Real Estate Market. Retrieved from https://www.citylab.com/life/2017/07/chinese-investmment-in-us-real-estate/534894/

Reuters. (n.d.). Chinese investment in London property is booming despite Brexit. Retrieved from https://www.businessinsider.com/r-hong-kong-property-investors-go-trophy-hunting-in-london-despite-brexit-2017-8

Saiidi, U. (2017, October 23). Here's why China is buying up assets in Australia. Retrieved from https://www.cnbc.com/2017/10/22/heres-why-china-is-buying-up-assets-in-australia.html

The Value of Education in Today's American Society: A Glimpse into the Current Way America Supports the Educational System – Athens State University. (n.d.). Retrieved from http://www.athens.edu/business-journal/spring-2013/the-value-of-education-in-todays-american-society-a-glimpse-into-the-current-way-america-supports-the-educational-system/

www.ingramcontent.com/pod-product-compliance
Lightning Source LLC
Chambersburg PA
CBHW070851050426
42453CB00012B/2130